HARVARD HISTORICAL MONOGRAPHS
III

PUBLISHED UNDER THE DIRECTION OF THE DEPARTMENT
OF HISTORY FROM THE INCOME OF

THE ROBERT LOUIS STROOCK FUND

LONDON : HUMPHREY MILFORD

OXFORD UNIVERSITY PRESS

The Federal Railway Land Subsidy Policy of Canada

by

JAMES B. HEDGES

Professor of History, Brown University

Cambridge

HARVARD UNIVERSITY PRESS

MCMXXXIV

CONTENTS

PREFACE

THE study which follows may properly be called a by-product. While engaged in a study of the land policies of the Canadian Pacific Railway, the writer found it necessary to inform himself concerning the railway land subsidy policy of the Dominion Government. He soon discovered, however, that little had been written upon the subject and that it was necessary to go to the documents themselves. Going through the records, at first merely with a view to obtaining a background, he became convinced that the subject was of such importance as to justify separate treatment, so that the investigation which in the beginning was but a means to another objective, became an end in itself.

While the chief emphasis of the work is necessarily upon the economic aspects of land subsidies, the political phase has not been neglected. In Canada, however, land grants to railways were never a political issue to the same extent as in the United States. The principle of subsidies in land was accepted in 1871 virtually without debate, with the result that subsequent discussion centered about the amount of land to be granted, and the recipients thereof. Nor were there present in Canada the constitutional and sectional questions which so beclouded and confused the issue in the United States.

The methods and practices employed by the Government in granting land to railways is one story—what the railways did with the land after acquiring it is quite another. Logically, they should be subjects

for separate discussion. A brief account of the disposition which the less important companies made of
their lands has been included here, however, in the belief that it shows one of the chief defects of the land
grant system, and also because the work of these roads
is not likely to be made the subject of special study.
The disposal of Canadian Pacific lands is of such importance that it requires treatment on a larger scale,
and, therefore, only passing mention has been made of
the broad outline of that Company's policies in this regard. The author hopes at a later date to assemble in
detailed form the complete record of the interesting
work which this company performed in the settlement
and development of the Canadian West.

Grateful acknowledgment is due to Mr. H. H.
Rowatt, Deputy Minister of the Interior, Ottawa, who
gave permission to examine the records of his Department, to Mr. Hugh M. Morrison for assistance rendered in numerous ways, and to the Social Science
Research Council, without whose grant-in-aid the completion of the work would not have been possible. Above
all, however, the writer wishes to express his appreciation of the unfailing kindness of Mr. H. E. Hume,
chairman of the Dominion Lands Board, Department
of the Interior, Ottawa, who not only gave him the
benefit of his unexcelled knowledge of the subject, but
also permitted free use of the great collection of documents assembled by him through years of patient labor.

J. B. H.

Providence, Rhode Island
April 21, 1934

THE FEDERAL RAILWAY LAND SUDSIDY
POLICY OF CANADA

CHAPTER I

The Evolution of the Policy

THE significance of governmental land policies in the settlement and development of the American and Canadian West is well understood. In outward appearance and general form, the land systems of the two countries have several points of similarity. Both governments rejected the revenue point of view in administering their public domains and, through the adoption of the homestead idea, committed themselves to the use of the land as an instrument of national development. Yet at the very moment that they were giving land directly to the individual settler, they were also giving it to railway companies in the form of subsidies. These two lines of action were distinctly at cross purposes, for the grants to the railways removed vast areas from the reach of the homesteader and forced the farmer to pay tribute to the corporation. The justification of these contradictory policies lay, of course, in the generally accepted belief that the building of railways increased the value of the settler's acres sufficiently to compensate for the few extra dollars which he paid for them. Of the soundness of this contention in many instances there can be little doubt. But in both the United States and Canada, before the race for railway subsidies had run its course, millions of acres of the finest lands available were in the hands of the transportation companies; and whatever the merits

3

or defects of carrying the principle of governmental
aid to railways to this extreme conclusion, the subsidies
themselves and the manipulation of them by the various
companies became important adjuncts of the general
land policies.

The subsidy system of the United States has been
the subject of frequent investigation, but that of Canada has been less thoroughly examined. This is unfortunate, for the colonization of the western lands of
the two countries, which was the by-product of their
land grant practices, was, in reality, one great movement rather than two. Settlers in search of desirable
lands knew no boundary lines; Americans migrated
into Canada and Canadians moved into the United
States. The great transcontinental railway companies
north and south of the border were managed with the
same ends in view, sometimes by men who had been
railway promoters on both sides of the forty-ninth
parallel. A study, therefore, which assembles the essential features of the Canadian subsidy policy, and
attempts to show not only its more obvious similarity
to that of the United States, but also the numerous
points of striking contrast, may help to serve as part
of the basis for a coordinated story of the westward
movement in a major portion of the North American
continent.

Adopting the land grant idea in the middle of the
last century, when the pioneer had but recently crossed
the Mississippi, the United States during the next
twenty years granted approximately 150,000,000
acres of land to western railways. So great was the
popular enthusiasm for railways in this period that no

price would have been thought too high for their construction, and it was easy enough to be lavish with the land of which there seemed to be an unlimited supply. Aside from the national importance of the projected lines, which was alleged in support of the grants to the Pacific railways, the chief argument in favor of land subsidies to railways in general was that which represented the Government as a private land-owner wishing to secure the largest possible return from his domain.[1] Much of the government land, however, was far from the settled portions of the country and would not sell unless the country could be developed. If a portion of this were given to a railway which would render the remaining lands salable, the Government would be acting in the enlightened manner of any intelligent land-owner. To emphasize this idea, the grants were to be made in alternate sections, with the price of the remaining lands doubled, so that the gain to the Government would be in direct and in exact proportion to the amount of the land granted.

As the building of the railways progressed and settlement advanced, the various transportation companies developed exploitive tendencies which irritated and alarmed the people of the West and culminated in the Granger movement. A general feeling of hostility toward the railways displaced the former manifestations of friendliness, and no amount of argument could convince the rebellious settler of the justice of the land subsidy policy. In the face of this opposition, grants

[1] J. B. Sanborn, *Congressional Grants of Land in Aid of Railways*, is the standard work on the origins of the land grant policy in the United States.

of land to railways became less frequent and by 1871 the practice was discontinued.

The year 1871, which marked the end of the subsidy era in the United States, began it in Canada. In that year the Conservative Government of Sir John Macdonald sponsored a proposal that a railway to the Pacific should be built by private enterprise, assisted by the Government with generous grants of land as well as of money. A series of events in the years just previous had brought the importance of a Pacific railway very much into the public mind. Soon after confederation was effected in 1867, rights to Rupert's Land were obtained from the Hudson's Bay Company. In 1871, British Columbia entered Confederation, but only at a price. Led by the redoubtable Alfred Waddington, the 10,000 inhabitants of that western province had demanded the construction of an overland highway to the Pacific. A greater challenge to a young nation of 4,000,000 souls could scarcely be imagined. To build a railway through the forbidding waste north of Lake Superior, across the uninhabited prairies and over the Rocky and Cascade barriers to tidewater was no mean achievement. As in the United States, the greatest asset in the accomplishment of such an undertaking was the land, and thus the origin of the land bounty system in Canada was inseparably bound up with the plans for the railway across the continent.

The proposal of the Macdonald Government provided, in addition to the grant of land, that construction should begin within two years and be completed within ten, a provision designed to satisfy the demands of British Columbia for the prompt construction of the railway. While the land grant idea was accepted by the Opposition, they protested that the country was unequal to the task of completing the enterprise in so short a period. But the Government refused to yield this point, although it did agree that the building of the road should not entail an increase in taxes in the Dominion.[2] This stipulation carried with it the implication that land was to be given on a large scale, since in no other way could an increase of the tax burden be avoided.

The Act of 1872,[3] which incorporated this proposal into law, provided for a grant of land not exceeding 50,000,000 acres to be appropriated in aid of the railway to the Pacific. The lands were to be located not more than twenty miles in depth, and not less than six nor more than twelve miles in frontage on the railway, the blocks to be so laid out that each one granted to the Company on one side of the railway should be opposite a block of like width reserved for the Government on the other side of the railway.[4]

The conveying of lands in large tracts was a distinct departure from the American practice of locating railway lands by alternate sections. Although open to

[2] *Journals of the House of Commons of the Dominion of Canada,* Session, 1871, pp. 197, 203, 264, and 268. The House resolved that the railway should be "constructed and worked by private enterprise . . . and that the public aid to be given . . . should consist of such liberal grants of land, and such subsidy in money, or other aid, not increasing the present rate of taxation, as the Parliament of Canada shall hereafter determine."

[3] Entitled "An Act respecting the Canadian Pacific Railway." *Statutes of Canada,* 35 Victoria, Cap. 71, assented to June 14, 1872.

[4] *Ibid.*

the objection that it almost certainly would lead to a less equitable division of the good and bad land between railway and Government, it was thought to be better suited to the conditions prevailing in the Canadian Northwest than the alternate section method. Under the latter system, it was said, there would be such a dispersion of homesteads in a given township as to retard community development and render difficult mutual assistance among the settlers, especially during the years prior to the sale of the intervening railway sections.[5] With large blocks available for homestead, however, compactness of settlement would result in the areas reserved for the Government.

While predicated upon Sir John Macdonald's original plan that the railway be built by private enterprise, the Act carried with it no definite provision for the actual construction of the road. If Canada had little of means and less of experience upon which to draw for such an undertaking, that was not true of the United States. American capitalists, with governmental bounties, had completed one railway to the Pacific and were projecting others. The enormous profits attending their efforts made them quick to recognize chances for similar fortunes elsewhere.

But while the Macdonald Government was not averse to accepting the aid and experience of American capital, political expediency demanded that Canadian interests be equally represented. One of the most prominent Canadian business men of the time was Sir

[5] As late as 1880-81 this argument was employed against the alternate section method. See *Debates of the House of Commons, 1880-81*, p. 331.

Hugh Allan, who controlled the Allan Steamship Line. Although primarily interested in water transportation, he had recently entered the railway business through his promotion of the North Shore road along the St. Lawrence, in competition with the Grand Trunk. If the assistance of Jay Cooke and his Northern Pacific associates, who had already indicated an interest in the undertaking, could be secured in cooperation with Sir Hugh, the question of American domination might be less of an issue. The negotiations between the Canadian and American capitalists moved smoothly enough, but before plans could be definitely shaped, strong opposition developed within the Dominion.

In Ontario, the presence of Sir Hugh Allan as one of a company to build the new railway meant that the terminus would be in Montreal rather than in Toronto. Moreover, in this province any suggestion of a possible affiliation with the Northern Pacific group was regarded with extreme suspicion. People there had no faith that the American promoters would not deliberately hamper the building of this Pacific railway to check competition with their own line. In Quebec, Sir George Cartier, a Cabinet member with a strong following among the French-speaking element, used his influence against Sir Hugh. As Cartier was closely associated with the Grand Trunk, the reasons for his position were obvious. With plenty of money available for purposes of propaganda, Allan won over Cartier and his supporters. But the opposition in Ontario was made of sterner stuff. A group of Toronto business men organized the Interoceanic Railway Company and petitioned the Government for a charter and aid for building a line of railway to the Pacific. They felt that their future security and prosperity were too closely interlocked with the Pacific railway to allow the building of it to fall into unsympathetic hands. All attempts which the Government made in the way of mergers and adjustments between the two contending groups were unsuccessful. After the Conservatives were reelected in 1872, an entirely new company, known as the Canadian Pacific, was organized, with a board of directors drawn from the various provinces and with the American capitalists excluded. Of this company Sir Hugh Allan was elected president.

Important to the story of the evolution of the Canadian land subsidy policy are some of the outstanding features of the charter granted to the Allan Company.[6] Thirty million dollars and 50,000,000 acres of land were offered in aid of the railway, on condition that no American interests should be admitted. The land was to be conveyed in the alternate blocks of the dimensions described in the Act of 1872, with an added provision to the effect that the Company "shall not be bound to receive any lands which are not of the fair average quality of the land in the sections of the country best adapted for settlement." [7] This was the first appearance of the idea that railway subsidy lands were to be of a certain designated quality, an idea which, as subsequent discussion will show, was to grow into a most important factor in the Canadian bounty system. Another clause of the charter, in regard to the price of the alternate blocks retained by the Government, stated

6 For the Charter, see *Sessional Papers* (No. 13), 1873.
7 *Ibid.*

that "unless the Company shall sell lands granted to them at a lower price, or shall otherwise agree, the Government shall for and during the term of twenty years . . . retain the upset price of such alternate blocks at an average price of not less than two dollars and fifty cents per acre." [8] It was openly charged in the Canadian Senate at the time that the Allan charter was copied from that of the Northern Pacific.[9] While this statement cannot be justified when applied to the charter as a whole, there can be no doubt that the plan proposed in the clause just quoted was borrowed from the Northern Pacific. It is noteworthy, however, that while in the United States it was the Government which insisted upon the double minimum as a justification for the land grant policy, in Canada it was the railway company which imposed the condition as a means of preventing the Government from underselling them.

But the terms of the Allan charter were never put into effect. As soon as the charter was granted, with its specific rejection of American participation, rumors purporting to come from disgruntled railway promoters in the United States were circulated to the effect that all was not strictly fair and above-board in the negotiations. There were those in Canada who did not quite believe it wholly fortuitous that Sir Hugh Allan was elected president of the new company, and who were willing to give credence to any sort of story. A steady undercurrent of dissatisfaction prevailed, and when the private correspondence of Sir Hugh was

[8] *Ibid.,* p. 20.
[9] See *Debates and Proceedings of the Senate of Canada,* First session, 2nd Parliament, 1873, p. 113. Statement by Mr. Campbell, April 18, 1873.

stolen and published, everyone was prepared to believe the worst.[10] The correspondence revealed that Cartier and Macdonald had made liberal use of Allan's money before the election of 1872. Out of this discovery grew the charge that the charter was the reward for services rendered, and that even the high office of prime minister had been degraded to this end. A political storm of the first magnitude resulted, and interest in all other issues was lost in the turmoil. A later and calmer survey of the whole affair reveals great indiscretion surely on the part of the Conservative leaders, but nothing much more than that. Sir Hugh had been a regular contributor to Conservative election funds for years. Moreover, he really gained nothing by the Conservative victory and the resulting charter except the assurance that the work in behalf of the railway would continue. Sir John Macdonald's indiscretion, too, was tempered by the very clear indication that he felt he was acting in the best interests of the Dominion.[11] But neither the Allan Company nor the Conservative Party was able to hold out against the attack at its height. The Company gave up its charter and the party went down to a smashing defeat at the hands of the Liberal Party, under the leadership of Alexander Mackenzie.

No government could have made its debut under more inauspicious conditions than that of Mackenzie. A country torn by political dissension and burdened with financial depression offered little of promise to

[10] For this correspondence, see *Journals of the House of Commons* (1873), Vol. VII.

[11] For Sir John Macdonald's defense of his position, see Pope, Joseph, *Memoirs of Sir John Macdonald,* Vol. II, pp. 174-189.

railway promotion, yet the Government showed no disposition to relax its efforts in that direction. As an inducement to private capital, Mackenzie offered $10,000 in cash and 20,000 acres of land per mile, in alternate blocks of twenty square miles, each block to have a frontage of not less than three nor more than six miles on the line of the railway.[12] Regardless of terms, however, private capital seemed unavailable and every offer went begging.

Discouraged in his efforts to interest a private company in the construction of the railway, Mackenzie resolved that the line should be built by the Government itself. The plan which he formulated with that end in view called for the completion of the links between navigable waterways, the abandonment, for the present at least, of the difficult portion north of Lake Superior, and British Columbia's consent to an extension of time for the finishing of the project. Mackenzie was completely unsuccessful in his attempts to win concessions from British Columbia, but he did make substantial progress in the location and construction of the road.

When the Conservatives were returned to power in 1878, Sir John Macdonald went forward for a time with the policy of government construction. In pursuance of this plan, Parliament adopted resolutions in 1879 appropriating 100,000,000 acres of land in aid of the railway.[13] These resolutions provided that all ungranted land within twenty miles of the railway

[12] *Statutes of Canada,* 27 Victoria, Cap. 14, assented to May 26, 1874.

[13] *Debates of the House of Commons,* 1879, pp. 1895-96, for the resolutions. For the vote on them see, *ibid.,* p. 1979.

should be used in satisfaction of this appropriation. If the lands adjoining the line of railway were not "of fair average quality for settlement," a substitute acreage was to be reserved in other portions of the prairie. The lands were to be vested in appointed commissioners, who were authorized to sell the land from time to time, and to invest the proceeds in government securities to be held for meeting the expenses of building the railway.

Beyond these very general provisions the resolutions of 1879 did not go, and it remained for the Department of the Interior to formulate a complete scheme for describing, setting aside, and selling this immense domain. Sir John Macdonald, in outlining such a plan, made direct reference to American policy, and used it as the basis of his proposal for handling the Canadian grant. In a memorandum of June 25, 1879,[14] after explaining the details of procedure in the United States, he expressed the belief that "a system somewhat similar . . . would be most convenient to adopt in administering the land grant of our own Railway." He would discard the large blocks, contemplated in earlier Canadian legislation upon the subject, in favor of the alternate sections of the United States, and would scrap the idea of reserving exclusively for sale all the lands along the railway, in favor of a system of free grants or homesteads distributed through the railway belt. Such free grants would not only silence the charges of land monopoly, but would also conduce to the sale of the intervening railway lands.

[14] This memorandum is to be found with *Order in Council* No. 976, June 28, 1879. (These are cited hereafter as *O. C.*)

Sir John estimated that in Manitoba and the north-west Territories there were, within 110 miles on either side of the railway, 125,000,000 acres of land, 100,-000,000 for the railway and the remainder for free grants. Land on each side of the railway he would divide into five belts: Belt A to extend back from the railway for five miles; Belt B, for fifteen miles beyond Belt A; Belts C and D, each for an additional twenty miles; and Belt E, stretching out for another fifty miles. In Belt A, all lands were to be sold at not less than $6 per acre. In the other Belts, four eighty-acre home-steads were allowed in the even-numbered sections, the remaining lands in such sections to be sold as pre-emptions at $1 to $2.50 per acre.[15] The odd-numbered sections in those Belts were railway lands, ranging in price from $5 per acre in Belt B to $1 per acre in Belt E.[16] Thus, except for Belt A, where all lands were reserved for the purpose of the railway, the alternate section idea was to prevail: odd-numbered sections for the railway, even-numbered for the Government.

This plan had scarcely been formulated, however, when a change in the American policy led to material modification of the Canadian regulations. Congress had increased from 80 to 160 acres the amount of land which could be homesteaded or preempted within the limits of a railway land grant. This change was be-

---

[15] O. C. No. 976, June 28, 1879, gave approval to the plan set forth in the memorandum of Sir John Macdonald. With the same Order in Council are to be found the detailed regulations for carrying the plan into effect. The title is "Regulations respecting the disposal of certain Dominion Lands for the purposes of the Canadian Pacific Railway," dated July 9, 1879.

[16] Ibid.

lieved to require "a corresponding alternation in the
area of Dominion lands proposed to be homesteaded
within the zone embracing Canadian Pacific Railway
lands, otherwise the manifestly superior advantages of
the United States over the Canadian policy would result in securing to the Western and Northwestern
States and Territories of the American Union all
European and other immigration for years to come." [17]
The need for change was considered the more urgent in
view of the exceedingly liberal conditions of sale offered
by the Northern Pacific and the St. Paul, Minneapolis,
and Manitoba Companies in the Northwest of the
United States, whose territory was in direct competition with that through which the Canadian Pacific was
to be built. As the Deputy Minister of the Interior
expressed it, "a rebate of one-half the purchase money
is made to persons who may have placed half the land
purchased, or in that proportion, under cultivation
within three years of the date of purchase, thus evi-
dencing the value which the Railway Companies attach
to actual settlement. It is presumed that the loss in
abatement of the purchase moneys under this system
is considered by the Companies as more than compen-
sated for by the additional traffic which the rapid
settlement of the country would bring to their roads." [18]
In view of these facts the Government increased from

[17] "Memorandum (confidential) by J. S. Dennis, Deputy Minister
of the Interior, to Sir John Macdonald, Minister of the Interior,"
July 3, 1879, with Ref. 20,088 on 18,909, Dominion Lands. It will
hereafter be understood that the manuscript material used in this
study is to be found in the Dominion Lands Branch of the Department
of the Interior, Ottawa.

[18] O. C. No. 1422, October 9, 1879; also O. C. No. 1461, October 24,
1879.

80 to 160 acres the homestead and preemption areas within the limits of the railway belts, and allowed in Belt A the same proportion of homesteads and preemptions as in the other belts.[10]

The resolutions of 1879 and the resulting regulations introduced significant changes in the land subsidy policy of the Dominion. The idea of the alternate section became definitely a part of the Canadian system, supplanting the original provision for large blocks. These regulations were devised with the assumption of continued governmental construction of the railway, but before they had received an adequate trial the plan for completion by the Government was abandoned in favor of another effort by private enterprise.

There were those in the Government, and out of it, who had not abandoned hope of having the railway built by capitalists. Sir Charles Tupper, the Minister of Railways and Canals, was one of these, and it was he who urged the Government to turn to a remarkable group of men who seemed to possess precisely the requirements needed for building the railway to the Pacific. These men, George Stephen, James J. Hill, Donald A. Smith, R. B. Angus, and John S. Kennedy, working together, had succeeded in converting the bankrupt St. Paul and Pacific road, in the United States, into a going concern. They had built this line to the Canadian boundary and had negotiated a traffic arrangement beyond to Winnipeg. In addition to this interest in an American company, several of the men were associated with important enterprises in Canada. This combination of successful railway promotion in

[19] *Ibid.*

the United States with a general understanding and knowledge of Canadian business and railway affairs was an ideal one. And the American venture had been a highly profitable one. If, reasoned Sir Charles Tupper, these men were planning to reinvest their profits, it was the part of wisdom for the Government to seek some sort of agreement with them. Tupper's counsel was heeded, negotiations were begun and carried through to a successful conclusion, and on October 21, 1880, the Syndicate Contract, under the terms of which the Canadian Pacific Railway was finally to be completed, was signed.

In December of the same year the contract was placed before Parliament for approval. Besides receiving the lines under construction by the Government, the Company, in return for building about 2,000 miles of railway, was to have a cash subsidy of $25,000,000 and a land grant of 25,000,000 acres.[20]   The Government promised freedom from rate regulation until the annual earnings on the capital of the Company reached ten per cent, with exemption from tariff duties on construction materials, from taxes on lands for twenty years, and from those on other property forever. As a guarantee against encroachments by rivals, no competitive lines connecting with the western states were to be chartered for a period of twenty years.

The terms of the contract were indubitably very favorable to the Company, but neither that fact nor the right and duty of the Opposition to oppose can justify the unreasoning attack which the Liberals launched

[20] For the provisions of the contract, see *Statutes of Canada,* 44 Victoria, Cap. 1 (1881).

against every provision of the agreement. So largely did the question become a political issue that it was impossible to consider any individual clause on its merits, and the unanimous disapproval of every item by the Liberals was the signal for an equally unanimous defense by the Conservatives.

Led by Edward Blake, the Opposition lost no opportunity for arousing the country against the contract. Another company, headed by Sir William Howland was hurriedly organized. This group offered to construct the road for $3,000,000 and 3,000,000 acres less than the Syndicate Contract required, and, as evidence of the genuineness of the offer, deposited a guarantee of $1,400,000. As further indication of good faith, it was prepared to pay duty on construction materials, and to waive the monopoly clause, the exemption from rate regulation, and the exemption from taxation. While the seemingly less onerous character of the offer of this company served as a strong talking point for the spokesmen of the Opposition, the Government professed to believe that the Liberals had organized the Company solely for political purposes. They could safely bring it forward at the eleventh hour, when there was no possibility that the Government would break the contract already signed.

Among the most pointed of the Liberal criticisms of the contract were those directed at the monopoly clause, which did so much to estrange the West from the East, and the exemption from taxation, which placed such a heavy burden upon the impecunious settlers in the West, a burden made heavier by the interpretation which rendered the lands exempt for twenty

years after the issuance of the patent. If the freedom
from regulation until ten per cent had been earned
seemed unduly favorable to the Company, it had been
anticipated in a clause of the General Railway Act,
while the exemption from duties on construction materials was justifiable, even if not consonant with the
"national policy" which the Conservatives had recently
adopted.

Probably no feature of the Liberal attack upon the
contract consumed more time or occasioned more bit-
terness than their denunciation of the alleged extravagance of the Government in trafficking away the
resources of the Dominion, and in this connection it is
the debate on the land subsidy which chiefly interests
us. Discussion of this subject began formally on December 13, 1880, when Sir Charles Tupper moved that
the House go into Committee of the Whole on the following Tuesday to consider resolutions affirming the
expediency of granting the $25,000,000 and the
25,000,000 acres of land provided for in the contract.[21]

The Liberals immediately trained their guns upon
the excessively generous provisions of the land subsidy.
Blake and his followers emphatically challenged the
validity of the Conservative boast of an advantageous
bargain with the Syndicate. Pointing out the disin-
genuous nature of the Government's claim to a saving
of from 25,000,000 to 75,000,000 acres, compared with
former land grant proposals, the Liberal leader asserted that if the value, rather than the amount, of the
land were considered, the subsidy was princely in its
proportions. The significant thing, in Blake's estima-

[21] *Debates of the House of Commons,* 1880-81, p. 48.

tion, was the location of the land, not the area.   Since
the Company was entitled to the alternate sections
within twenty-four miles on either side of the railway,
the value of its land was far in excess of any similar
area elsewhere in the west.   Ridiculing the Conservative
estimate of $1 per acre as the value of the land, Blake
used their own earlier prices to prove that the figure
was absurdly low.[22]   In terms of the land regulations
instituted by the Macdonald Government in 1879, the
bulk of the Canadian Pacific land grant would fall in
Belts A and B, where the prices were $6 and $5 per
acre respectively.[23]   It was the land sixty miles or more
from the railway which those regulations had priced
at $1 an acre.

Continuing their attack, the Opposition made much
of the contrast between the enormous area the Canadian
Pacific was to receive and the much smaller grants
made to the railways in the United States.   One Liberal member had computed the average grant to the
American railways, exclusive of the Pacific roads, to
be 3,790 acres per mile, while the Syndicate was to
have almost 13,000 acres for each mile of construction.[24]   Even the Northern Pacific, the most generously
endowed of the lines in the United States, might not obtain more than 15,000,000 acres of arable land.

Nor did the Liberals fail to stress the adverse effects
which such a large subsidy would have upon the whole
course of settlement in the West.   Canada, it was observed, must compete with the United States for immi-

---

[22] *Debates of the House of Commons,* 1880-81, p. 79.
[23] *Ibid.,* p. 80.
[24] *Ibid.,* p. 792.

grants, which it could not hope to do successfully unless able to "offer conditions at least equal to those offered by the United States." [25] On this point the contract contained no clause satisfactory to the Opposition. Without any reservation whatever, it ceded to the Syndicate 25,000,000 acres of land, the most fertile and best situated in the Northwest. Because of the alternate section plan, not only the railway lands, but the Crown lands as well, would be at the mercy of the Company. Fifty million acres, more than could possibly be sold within a quarter of a century, would be subject to the arbitrary whim of a private syndicate.[26] The latter would have it in its power to paralyze the efforts of the Government to settle and develop the West. If, for purposes of speculation, or for other reasons, the Company should withhold its lands from sale, the Government would be powerless to sell and colonize its own lands. In each of the government sections within the railway belt there were to be two homesteads and two preemptions—in other words, two settlers.[27] Should the railway section not be sold, the occupant of the government section would be forced not only to "keep up his roads and his fences, but the roads and fences of the neighboring lot," and he would be obliged "to pay double municipal and school taxes." As the Opposition viewed the situation, few would be disposed to purchase the government sections unless those of the railway were sold at the same time, and the

[25] *Ibid.,* p. 738.

[26] *Debates of the House of Commons,* 1880-81, p. 738.

[27] It was assumed that the homesteader would buy the adjoining preemption lot.

surest way to expedite sales by the Syndicate was to
set a time limit for the disposal of its lands, thereby ren-
dering it impossible for sections to be deliberately held
in the hope that the expenditure of labor and capital
by the settler on the Crown lots would enhance the value
of the adjoining railway land.

Fortunately for the Liberal argument, there seemed
to be ample precedent for the establishment of such a
time limit for the sale of railway lands. The Conservative Government having adopted the Union Pacific
Railroad in the United States as a standard for the
construction of the Canadian Pacific, there was no reason why the Opposition should not employ the same
road as a criterion of land subsidy practice. Accordingly, they seized upon the clause of the Union Pacific
charter which required that subsidy lands not sold
within ten years after the completion of the road should
be open to occupation and preemption like other lands
at not less than $1.25 per acre.[28] The fact that this
clause had not been enforced against the Union Pacific
in no way diminished its effectiveness as an argument
against the land subsidy. But, while making much of
the absence of such a guarantee in the Canadian Pacific
contract, the Liberals attempted no inclusion of a definite time limit in the document. Instead, they sought
to achieve the same end by other means. The Opposition insisted it was only fair that the Government should
officially place a price on the land, in order that the
entire country might know definitely as to the monetary
value of the aid extended to the Syndicate.[29] If a

[28] *Debates of the House of Commons,* 1880-81, p. 739.
[29] *Debates of the House of Commons,* 1880-81, p. 739.

value of $1 per acre was assigned the land, in accordance with the estimate of the Minister of Railways, then the Company ought to be forced to sell at that maximum. In the event the Company was unwilling to sell the land for less than $2 to $3 an acre, it would be the duty of the Government either to give a considerably "less amount than 25,000,000 acres, or take before Parliament and before the people the responsibility of giving to the Syndicate lands valued by the Syndicate and by the Government at $50,000,000 or $75,-000,000." [30] The Liberals sponsored an amendment, therefore, requiring that a maximum price be placed on the land, thereby depriving the Company of every incentive to retard the settlement of the West by holding the land for appreciation in value. But, like all other attempts to change the contract, this was voted down by a strict party vote of 49 to 118.[31]

If the Opposition was unable to see anything good in the terms of the agreement, the Conservatives were equally incapable of finding any defects in it. On their side, much of the burden of defending the provisions of the contract devolved upon Sir Charles Tupper. As Minister of Railways and Canals, it was his duty to expound the document to the House, and, in this case, to expound was but to justify its every clause. Tupper largely anticipated the objections of the Liberals, and he very cleverly sought to confound them out of their own mouths. By presenting an imposing array of their earlier statements in regard to land and land grants, utterly inconsistent with their

[30] *Ibid.*
[31] *Ibid.*, p. 740.

current comments, he made their criticisms appear
patently captious, partisan, and void of sincerity. Replying to Liberal assertions as to the great value of
western lands, he quoted Blake as having in 1875
ridiculed the idea that land for the Georgian Bay
branch was worth $2 an acre.[32]   Blake had then
thought that $1 per acre was more reasonable. Very
appropriately, Tupper could point out that during the
six-year interval nothing had happened to increase the
value to $3.18 per acre, the value the Opposition was
now attaching to the land in the West. Tupper made
equally effective use of earlier speeches of Alexander
Mackenzie expressing the belief that the competition
of the free lands of the United States would prevent the
sale of the Canadian lands at more than $1 per acre.[33]

No less inconsistent were the Liberal complaints in
regard to the amount of land granted by the contract.
As the Conservatives pointed out, the Allan charter
had called for a grant of 50,000,000 acres, while the
Mackenzie Government in 1874 had offered 54,000,000
acres to any company which would build the railway.
Thus, as compared with the Opposition proposal, the
terms of the contract actually saved the country 29,-
000,000 acres.   Far from being extravagant, the
Conservatives were husbanding the resources of the
Dominion. The resolutions of Parliament in 1879 had
pledged 100,000,000 acres in support of the railway;
the Government was using just one quarter of this
amount.[34]

[32] *Ibid.*, p. 63.
[33] *Debates of the House of Commons,* 1880-81, p. 63.
[34] *Ibid.*, p. 70.

Liberal fears of a great land monopoly in the West, the Conservatives alleged, were wholly groundless. Instead of "locking up" 54,000,000 acres in large blocks, as the Liberals had sought to do under the Act of 1874, the contract locked up but 25,000,000 acres in alternate sections. While under the Allan charter the Government was obliged not to sell its lands for less than $2.50 an acre, the Syndicate agreement made it possible to give away the remaining lands if the public interest so required.[35]   "No policy," Tupper said, "did the Syndicate press more strongly upon us than that of settling the land as fast as we could. They say we should be only too glad to plant a free settler upon every acre belonging to the Government."

Nor would the Company withhold its lands from sale for speculative or other reasons. The surest guarantee against such a course was the zeal which the members of the Syndicate had displayed in settling the lands of the St. Paul and Pacific in Minnesota. Fortunate it was for Canada that the experience gained there would now be brought to the colonization of the Canadian prairies. The entire history of railway land subsidies, the Conservatives asserted, was a refutation of the land monopoly charge of their opponents. The Company must sell the land and bring a population into the country in order to sustain the road. The land grant railways of the United States had incurred large expenditures in promoting the sale of their lands, the Atchison, Topeka, and Santa Fe having spent $.88 per acre for that purpose.[36]   The "glass cases and jars

35 *Ibid.*
36 *Debates of the House of Commons,* 1880-81, p. 537.

containing wheat, corn and other products of the Western States," which were on exhibition at every railway station, were the work of the railways, not of the United States Government. Surely nothing less was to be expected of the men who were to build the Canadian Pacific through an uninhabited wilderness. The Company would expend from nine to ten millions in the cause of immigration, which, in turn, would relieve the Dominion Government of that expense.

After weeks of debate, in which the contending forces exhausted every argument, and in the course of which the twenty-three amendments offered by the Liberals were voted down with monotonous regularity, the contract with the Syndicate was finally approved by a straight party vote. With that vote, the Canadian Pacific Railway approached one step nearer to reality, while the railway land subsidy policy of the Canadian Government became a fact rather than a theory.

One who compares the political aspect of railway land subsidies in the United States and Canada cannot fail to be impressed by two important differences. Canada was not troubled by the constitutional issue which proved so vexatious in the United States. In the Dominion there could, of course, be no question as to the constitutional right of Parliament to vote land subsidies in aid of railways. In the United States, on the other hand, there were those who had genuine doubt as to whether the Constitution warranted such grants by Congress, and there were many more who seized upon the constitutional argument as a means of cloaking base and selfish motives. In Canada, likewise, the debates attending the adoption of the land grant policy fail to reveal the sectional cleavage which bulked so large with her neighbor to the south.

In one respect, however, the political history of land subsidies in the two countries is similar: in neither was the principle of railway land grants a party issue. While it was a Conservative Government which signed the contract with the Syndicate, the subsidy idea had been adopted years before, and the Mackenzie Government in the seventies had been committed to that principle. And, despite the opposition of the Liberals to the Syndicate Contract, their quarrel was with the specific provisions of the grant rather than with the principle. That the Howland Company, which the Opposition supported, offered to build the railway for 22,000,000 acres of land represents a difference in degree rather than in kind.

CHAPTER II

AFTER ten years of discussion and political controversy, a definite plan for the handling of land subsidies had been formulated and the Canadian Pacific Syndicate, fortified with a promise of 25,000,000 acres of land, assumed the tremendous responsibility of completing the transcontinental railway. The land provisions of the Syndicate Contract were the product of various developments. Although there had never been much doubt in Canada as to the wisdom of using the land for the building of railways, there had been considerable uncertainty as to the best manner of using it. Here the basic principle of conveying land by alternate sections, which had been so consistently employed in the United States, was not at first accepted. The earlier proposals made in Dominion councils had contemplated the granting of land in large blocks, a procedure which, had it been put into effect, would have been so complete a departure from the American method as to leave little in common between the two, save the simple fact that both had given land in aid of railways. When the alternate section plan was written into the agreement with the Company which was undertaking the building of a railway across the continent, a very significant point of contrast was removed, and the common use by both countries of this method of land conveyance has

29

led to the assumption that the railway land subsidy policy of Canada was "transplanted bodily" from the United States.[1]   But to accept a similarity in one feature, however fundamental, as indicating a resulting parallel in growth and development would lead to quite erroneous conclusions, and would leave out of account the more interesting phase of the Canadian land grant system. Granting a railway company 25,000,000 acres of land was one thing; locating and selecting it was another. The land bounty had been won only after a sharp political battle, with all the attendant publicity, but the lands were set aside and located through administrative regulations, Orders in Council and Acts of Parliament, all of which largely escaped public notice. A study of these documents, however, reveals the policy of the Canadians taking unusual departures from American practice and makes of it not a slavish imitation, but an original creation, developed along new lines dictated by their own peculiar needs and circumstances.

At the outset, one clause of the Syndicate Contract contained a provision which, when put into operation, afforded endless opportunity for the growth of a subsidy policy unique in character. This clause, which became known as the "fairly fit for settlement" clause, read: "if any such sections consist in a material degree of land not fairly fit for settlement, the company shall not be obliged to receive the same as part of the grant." [2]

[1] For such a view, see Samuel E. Moffett, *The Americanization of Canada,* New York, 1907, p. 75.
[2] For the contract, see *Statutes of Canada,* 44 Victoria, Cap. 1 (1881).

Here was a regulation which, followed to its logical conclusion, meant that the Company need not accept any 25,000,000 acres of the wilderness which was then the Canadian West, but that it could, in a sense, pick and choose, a privilege not granted to the subsidized lines in the United States. This "fit for settlement" idea had appeared before in Canadian records. A similar provision had been part of the Allan charter. It had come to light again in the Act of 1874 and in the resolutions of 1879. But there is every reason to believe that the political exponents of the subsidy plan gave scant attention to the real significance of such a clause. It was only when the debate on the Syndicate Contract was approaching an end that reference was made to this stipulation, and then the discussion was in no sense commensurate with the importance of the subject. There is little to indicate that either side regarded the clause with any concern, other than as something to attack or defend in a political discussion. However, the persistence with which the idea had been injected into Canadian land grant legislation is evidence that although the politicians were largely unmindful of its significance, there were others who were not. Sir Hugh Allan's associates were men of the Northern Pacific, while the Syndicate group was in control of an American land grant railway. Here were men who knew at first hand the workings of land subsidies in the United States; who knew what pitfalls to avoid and what concessions to obtain, and it seems reasonable to suppose that the "fairly fit for settlement" clause was a result of their experience.

Another significant provision of the Syndicate Con-

tract created an additional problem in locating the
25,000,000 acres to which the Company was entitled.
Lands were to be granted to the Company only in the
region popularly known as the "fertile belt." [3]   As the
name implies, this section of Canada, extending from
Winnipeg to Jasper House, was at the time regarded
as the most attractive portion of the West.   For the
900 miles of railway to be built through this part of
the prairie, the Company was to receive lands in alternate sections within twenty-four miles on each side of
the railway, creating what was subsequently known as
the forty-eight mile, or main line, belt.   But over the
lands of Ontario and British Columbia, the Dominion
Government had no control.   While it is true that the
latter province had in 1871 transferred to the Dominion a twenty-mile belt on either side of a Pacific
railway, the Canadian Pacific Syndicate had refused to
accept this land as part of its subsidy.   For constructing the railway through the thousand miles of Lauren-
tian rocks and muskeg wastes, and across the rugged
mountains of those two provinces, therefore, the Canadian Pacific must also receive its reward in the
"fertile belt."   This provision worked no hardship on
the Company, as it was in reality an added guarantee
of a good selection of land, but it did complicate the
problem of locating a large grant already conditioned
by the "fit for settlement" requirement.   Any railway
in the United States would doubtless have welcomed a
gift of the fertile lands of Illinois and Iowa in return
for pushing a line across the Rockies, but Congressional
restrictions allowed no such privileges.   Numerous as

[3] *Ibid.*

were the legal loop-holes through which the wily American railway promoter might make his way to greater profits, he found that in this one respect the law could not be easily circumvented. The subsidies in the United States, providing as they did for stipulated amounts of land per mile along the entire length of the line, carried no guarantee as to the quality of the land. All American land grant roads received certain undesirable lands, while the transcontinental lines found themselves in possession of vast areas, either totally worthless or valuable only for grazing purposes. The Canadian Pacific, in attempting to avoid the acquisition of lands of such low quality, thrust upon the Dominion Government a heavy burden of responsibility. It was soon to become evident that the administration of the Canadian Pacific grant was not the simple matter of conceding automatically a certain number of acres for each completed mile of rails, as had been true in the United States, but the more difficult one of finding 25,000,000 acres of land, part of it along the railway, part of it elsewhere in the "fertile belt," but all of it measuring up to the Company's standard of land "fairly fit for settlement."

The subsidy was to be administered through the Department of the Interior. The general provisions were simple. For convenience in conveying the lands to the Company as portions of the line were completed, the railway was divided into two sections, eastern and central. As each twenty miles of track were laid, the Government was to convey the lands at a stipulated acreage per mile according to location in the eastern or central section. The alternate sections tributary to the main

line, limited as they were to the "fertile belt," would
not satisfy the total amount of the grant. This shortage, according to the contract, was to be made up from
other lands on the prairie, between the 49th and 57th
parallels. Here the Company might, with the consent
of the Government, select lands in the "alternate sections extending back 24 miles on each side of any branch
line or lines of railway to be located by the Company . . .
or of any common front line or lines agreed upon between
the government and the Company." [4] The lands so
located along branch lines were to be part of the main
line subsidy, and it was assumed that in this manner
any deficiency could be overcome. In theory, then, all
of the lands granted were to be alternate sections directly tributary either to the main or branch lines, but
in actual practice the Company, in searching for lands
"fairly fit for settlement," went far afield and eventually
found itself with millions of acres far removed from
either main or branch lines, with grants to other companies frequently intervening between these reserves
and the Company right-of-way.

The work of building the railway was inaugurated
very soon after the approval of the contract, and with
equal promptness beginnings were made in the for-
midable task of securing title to the land. The general
financial policy of the Syndicate group was a conservative one. The directors of the Company sought to build
their road without resorting to the enormous bonded
indebtedness which had characterized most railways on
the continent. It was perhaps because of this conservative fiscal program that such persistent and vigor-

[4] *Ibid.*

ous attention was given to the acquisition of the lands granted to the railway. The ultimate financial success of the venture depended in no small measure on the immense resources which would be gained through the sale and development of the subsidy lands. That vigilance was necessary, is attested by the fact that not until twenty-two years after the contract became law, and seventeen years after the completion of the railway, was the last acre finally set aside for the Company. The need for alertness was increased with the appearance in the early eighties of numerous smaller railway companies for whom millions of acres were reserved, first for purchase, later as subsidies. As to the soundness of the Canadian Pacific's later contention that these grants violated the spirit of the Syndicate Contract, there may be reasonable doubt; that the wholesale and indiscriminate manner in which Ottawa authorized land bounties to the lesser railways added greatly to the difficulty of finding the land for the Canadian Pacific, and forced the Company to adopt an apparently aggressive policy for the protection of its interests there can, however, be no question.

As the construction of the road moved forward, the Company acquired at various times four large land reserves, far removed from the main line belt. The establishment of these reserves was pressed in each case by the railway as part of its consistent effort to protect itself against governmental delay in reserving and conveying the lands. Once land subsidies became the accepted policy, the Canadian Pacific was not alone in petitioning the Government, and it was quite possible for much valuable land to be turned to other uses before enough rails could be laid to claim the entire grant.

The first of the land reserves was obtained during the second year of construction. In January, 1882, 161 miles of the main line had been constructed from Winnipeg westward, and the Pembina Mountain Branch had been located.[5] On the basis of this construction, actual and anticipated, the Company requested and secured the location and conveyance of the lands already earned along the main line and along the located branch to the south.[6] A request made at the same time, however, for the reservation of an additional tract of land extending south from the proposed branch line to the international boundary was refused. But the Company was not content to accept a first refusal as final. Engineers and surveyors had been at work, and a few convincing figures were at hand. The most generous estimate of land available in the forty-eight mile belt placed the total at only 6,000,000 acres. Great additional tracts must come from other portions of the West, if the entire grant was to be realized. Immigration into the Northwest was too scattered and too uncertain to justify the projection of enough branch lines in that territory to make up the deficit. Against the time when colonization should be more stable and conditions more propitious for railway expansion, the Company felt the need of some form of guarantee of

[5] See letter of A. M. Burgess, Secretary, Department of the Interior, to Charles Drinkwater, Secretary, C. P. R. Co., March 14, 1882, File No. 34187-2. In this letter Burgess refers to and summarizes various letters from the C. P. R. on the subject, especially Drinkwater's letter of January 13, 1882.

[6] *Ibid.*

land in the North.[7]   The Government was eventually
persuaded of the justice of the Company's request, and
the first northern reserve was created.[8]   This reserve,
between the 52nd and 54th degrees of latitude and the
104th and 116th degrees of longitude, contained some
of the finest land in the Dominion.   Here, it was estimated, the odd-numbered sections would yield 19,-
000,000 acres which, after deducting the lands unfit
for settlement, would guarantee the Company one-half
the total grant.[9]

Successful in its first efforts, the Company was
not slow in making another attempt to secure a reserve
in the South.   There was more possibility of immediate
revenue from land south of the railway, where settlement and development had already begun, than in the
lands to the North, whatever their potential value.   In
requesting this additional allotment the Company advanced perfectly plausible arguments.   The first estimate of 6,000,000 acres available in the forty-eight
mile belt along the main line had been reduced to a
scant 5,000,000 as the surveying proceeded.[10]   Moreover, many of the sections from Winnipeg to the western boundary of Manitoba were already privately
owned, and therefore not available for the land subsidy.[11]   The Minister of the Interior acceded to the
Company's request that the apparent shortage be made

[7] O. C. No. 2099, October 24, 1882, which relates the view of the
Company.

[8] Ibid.

[9] Ibid.

[10] O. C. No. 2152, November 3, 1882, in which these facts are set
forth.

[11] Ibid.

up from lands to the south. Arrangements were made
for a reserve of approximately 2,500,000 acres between
the original western boundary of Manitoba and the
Coteau or Dirt Hills.[12] The land lay between the
southern limit of the forty-eight mile belt along the
main line of the Canadian Pacific and the northern
limit of a belt previously reserved for the Manitoba
Southwestern Colonization Railway.[13] A few months
later the reserve was extended to include all of the odd-
numbered sections of land still at the disposal of the
Government, between the forty-eight mile belt and the
49th parallel, and between the Red River and the
original western limit of Manitoba.[14] This enlarged
Southern or International Boundary Reserve, like the
one in the North, was too far from the main line to be
directly developed by it. Both were too remote to
contribute in a substantial manner to the growth of
the traffic of the railway. The two reserves, however,
were dependable assets of a company embarking upon
an undertaking of great magnitude. They guaranteed
the larger portion of the grant, assured the Canadian
Pacific of a significant influence in the future development of the country, and afforded a measure of control
over rival transportation enterprises.

In the nineties, two additional reserves were obtained in partial satisfaction of the main line grant.
The first of these, known as the Lake Dauphin Reserve,
was secured ostensibly in connection with the building

[12] *Ibid.*

[13] The lands reserved for the M. S. W. Col. Ry. were to be purchased at $1 per acre. It appears, however, that they were not ac-
quired by the Railway.

[14] *O. C.* No. 110, January 25, 1883.

of a line of railway referred to as the Lake Dauphin
Extension of the Selkirk Branch.[15]   Projected in 1891,
this branch had been "surveyed and located within the
meaning of clause 11 of the original Contract of
1881," which provided for the granting of lands along
the branch lines for the purposes of the main line
subsidy. Accordingly, the Company asked for the odd-
numbered sections within twenty-four miles of the proposed branch line. In addition, it petitioned for other
lands, to be used as reserves against probable deficiencies
in the statutory belt along this line. The fertile and
highly desirable lands in the Swan River district were
suggested as a possibility. It was estimated that some
250,000 acres of land "fairly fit for settlement" were
available there.[16]   To the east and south, between the
grant of the Manitoba and North-Western Railway
Company and the belt appertaining to the Lake Dauphin Branch, was a similar area of suitable land.[17]
Prior commitments by the Government, however, made
it impossible for the Canadian Pacific to acquire all of
this acreage. Much of the land had been reserved since
1885 for the Winnipeg Great Northern Railway, one
of the various colonization roads which followed on the
heels of the Canadian Pacific.[18]   The Government did
agree, however, to the allotment of a smaller reserve,
and set aside the odd-numbered section still at the disposal of the Dominion within a belt of twenty-four miles

[15] *O. C.* No. 414, February 18, 1895, sets forth the facts in connection with this line.

[16] Charles Drinkwater, Secretary, C. P. R. Co., to John R. Hall,
Secretary, Department of the Interior, June 27, 1894, File 34187-8.

[17] *Ibid.*

[18] *O. C.* No. 414, February 18, 1895.

on either side of the Lake Dauphin Branch from the point where it left the western limit of the Winnipeg Great Northern Reserve to its terminus.[19]

With the way closed to the acquisition of a really large tract of land in closer proximity to its own lines, the Company turned once again to the far Northwest. In this region the Government reserved for it the odd-numbered sections between the 4th and 5th meridians of the Dominion land surveys and the 54th and 55th parallels of latitude.[20] The land, subsequently designated as the Second Northern Reserve, was situated to the east and northeast of Edmonton, so far removed from the main line of the railway that there would be slight chance of any real colonization for many years to come.

These reserves were not administered without many conflicts of opinion between the two parties to the agreements. One long and serious controversy developed which altered materially the character of the original grant. At an early date in the construction of the railway, the Company had been forced to borrow heavily from a Conservative government genuinely anxious lest the project which it had sponsored should result in failure. In 1886 there remained on the Company's books a balance of $9,880,912, with interest, on a loan of $29,880,912. Funds were not available to meet this balance, and the Company turned to its only tangible asset, the land already given by Ottawa.

[19] *O. C.* No. 414, February 18, 1895.
[20] *O. C.* No. 3613, December 18, 1895. As Annex "B" to this Order in Council is the letter from Charles Drinkwater, Secretary, C. P. R. Co., to T. Mayne Daly, Minister of the Interior, asking that these lands be reserved for the Company.

By an agreement of March 30th of that year, the railway guaranteed to the Government the relinquishment of an area of land which, valued at $1.50 per acre, would approximate the amount of the unpaid debt.[21] This reduction of the land grant by 6,793,014 acres was to be effected, in the words of the statute, "by the retention by the Government of land of equal average quality and value with the lands constituting the portion of the Company's land grant not heretofore disposed of by the Company." [22]

For several years no actual steps were taken toward the execution of the covenant. During those years the Company worked steadily at the examination of the lands within the forty-eight mile belt and in southern Manitoba. By January, 1889, it had actually accepted 6,524,000 acres, which it had set forth in detailed schedules, and it estimated, on the basis of available information, that it would eventually find in these two areas enough suitable land to bring the total to approximately 8,350,000 acres. This would leave some 16,650,000 acres to be accounted for. Interpreting the agreement of March 30, 1886 to be merely a reduction of 6,793,014 acres in the total acreage to which they were entitled, the Company, by the simple subtraction of that amount from the 16,560,000 acres, arrived at an estimate of the area which remained to be selected. Its assumption was that it was free to appropriate this balance of some 9,850,000 acres from

21 The agreement, together with the Act of Parliament approving it, is to be found in *Statutes of Canada,* 49 Victoria, Cap. 9, assented to June 2, 1886.
22 *Ibid.*

the best lands available in its First Northern Reserve. To this end, it projected a series of branch lines into that region, each line to be the means of developing a particular area, and to carry with it the alternate sections to a distance of twenty-four miles on either side of the road.[23] By thus locating the lands to which it was entitled in the North, the Company would be certain of serving them with its own lines, thereby reducing the dangers of competition to a minimum.

But while the Government and the Company could agree on the efficacy and value of branch lines, on the question of locating land for the railway along these proposed northern extensions, they were at loggerheads. Here the interpretation of the agreement of land relinquishment of 1886 became of the utmost significance. Canadian Pacific officials held the view, as previously indicated, that the agreement had effected nothing more than a reduction in the total area to which they were entitled.[24] The Government, on the other hand, was equally firm in the opinion that there must be actual relinquishment by the Company of lands of quality and value equal to those retained. It is easy to see the advantages which would accrue to the Company if its interpretation was accepted.

The Government, however, was not easily persuaded. The Minister of the Interior, in a communication to

[23] Charles Drinkwater, Secretary, C. P. R. Co., to John R. Hall, Secretary, Department of the Interior, January 17, 1889, File No. 34187-7.

[24] Memorandum by E. Dewdney, Minister of the Interior, March 11, 1890, with O. C. No. 863, May 20, 1890, in which he refers to the discussions and correspondence between the Company and the Government.

the Cabinet in regard to the controversy, made a clear-cut statement of the Government's stand. He recommended "that the Company be definitely informed that the government is not in a position to deal with the Company in regard to the residue of the subsidy to which they are entitled on the basis that the arrangement of 1886 amounted to no more than a reduction of the acreage originally intended to be granted to the Company, and that the government will require in fulfillment of the said arrangement that out of the land that would have been available for the gross subsidy, a portion sufficient to yield to the government for the purpose above mentioned, 6,793,014 acres, shall be set apart and freed from all claims by the Company in respect of the subsidy promised in the original contract." [25]

In suggesting the basis of an equitable plan for the release of the lands by the Canadian Pacific, the Minister referred to the report regarding the amount and value of the lands reserved in the North for the Company, which had already been prepared by the Department of the Interior. The report showed that the tract contained the very best land in the Territories and that nowhere else in the Northwest could there have been found a block of equal area and fertility. Of 1,057 townships surveyed by the Department, 641 were of the finest quality, with only six townships totally unsuited for farming. Of the unsurveyed portions of the reservation, the land along the Saskatchewan was fertile, with an abundance of timber; that to the

[25] Memorandum by E. Dewdney, Minister of the Interior, March 11, 1890, with *O. C.* No. 863, May 20, 1890.

north and east of Battleford was favorably known; while the Carrot River Valley had an excellent reputation. "Everything considered," observed the Minister, "a very close approximation as to character and value will be obtained by assuming for the whole of the reservation the same proportions of the several kinds of land as are found in the surveyed districts." On the basis of this assumption, the odd-numbered sections of the Northern Reserve would contain about 19,-000,000 acres of farming land, of which almost 12,000,000 would be of the very finest quality.[26] After deducting ten per cent for water, Indian Reserves, etc., there would remain over 17,000,000 acres "fairly fit for settlement."

The Department of the Interior recommended as a solution of the difficulty that the Northern Reserve be divided into two equal parts, taking the 110th meridian of longitude, which was the 4th meridian in the Dominion Lands system of surveys, as the dividing line.[27] The Canadian Pacific should relinquish to the Government that portion of the reserve to the east of this line of demarcation. But, in order to protect the rights of the Dominion and to provide land subsidies for other railways, should such be deemed desirable, there was to be added to this eastern portion the adjoining land to the south of the 52nd parallel, and extending to the South Saskatchewan River and to northern limits of the forty-eight mile belt of the Canadian Pacific.[28]

[26] *Ibid.*
[27] *Ibid.*
[28] The precise description of the tract thus added was the area "bounded on the north by the 52nd parallel of latitude, on the east by the 104th degree, and on the west by the 110th degree of longitude,

The added area was likewise to be released from all claims in respect of the land subsidy of the railway company which might subsequently be advanced.[29] This secured not only an equal division of the land from the point of view of area, but also from that of value. The advantage of fertility of soil and proximity to markets and centers of population enjoyed by the eastern part would be counterbalanced by the superior climate and admirable distribution of timber and water in the western part.

By an additional provision, the Canadian Pacific secured a return of approximately 1,000,000 acres of the land yielded to the Government. The ultimate attractiveness of the Government's portion of the reservation would be enhanced by the completion of the Qu'Appelle, Long Lake, and Saskatchewan Railway, which was then projected northward from Regina. It was deemed desirable from the point of view of public interest that the Canadian Pacific should build a branch from a point on this line, at or near Saskatoon, to the navigable waters of the North Saskatchewan River. To encourage early construction, the Government proposed to grant to the Company from the lands just released, a belt of territory stretching from the southern boundary of the reservation, in a northwesterly direction to the 110th meridian, and to a width of

on the south by the South Saskatchewan River from the said 110th degree of longitude till it intersects the northern boundary of the 48 mile belt of the Main line of the C. P. R." *Ibid.*

[29] Since this additional area had not been reserved for the Canadian Pacific, this last provision evidently was designed as a safeguard against any request which the Company might make in the future.

twenty-four miles.[30]   Such a block would yield in odd-
numbered sections about 1,000,000 acres, which would
constitute not an additional subsidy, but rather a portion of the main line grant.   A common front line was
to be established, as provided by the eleventh clause of
the contract of 1881, but the lands were to be reserved
to a depth of only twelve miles on either side instead
of the twenty-four miles which the contract had called
for.   Such an arrangement was considered mutually
advantageous.   In this way the Government would
secure railway facilities for this eastern portion of the
reservation, without relinquishing its claim to too great
an area, while the Canadian Pacific would receive land
tributary to a branch line which it would probably
build in any event.

By an Order in Council of May 20, 1890, these
recommendations of the Minister of the Interior were
approved,[31] and on January 7, 1891, were incorporated
into an agreement between the Government and the
Canadian Pacific Company.   All lands in the area east
of the 110th meridian were released to the Government
immediately; lands in the western portion of the reservation not selected by January 1, 1892, were to be
opened to settlement after that date.[32]   The line of
railway from Saskatoon to the North Saskatchewan
River was to be constructed in return for the 1,000,000
acres reserved for that purpose, the area known thereafter as the Battleford Block.[33]

[30] Dewdney's Memorandum of March 11, 1890; *loc. cit.*
[31] *O. C.* No. 863, May 20, 1890.
[32] For the text of the agreement, see Ref. 255263 on 51724.
[33] *Ibid.*

The Company, although forced to yield to the Government's interpretation of the relinquishment, accepted the final adjustment as an equitable disposition of the controversy. Perhaps a company less in the public eye might have succeeded in persuading the Government of the justice of its point of view. But the political controversy over the original contract had been too heated for the Conservative Party to allow any charges of undue leniency towards the Canadian Pacific to be brought against it.

As a result of the agreement, the proposed branch lines through the Northern Reserve were abandoned. Development of some of the lands to have been served by these lines was later made possible through the construction of the roads eastward from Lecombe and Wetaskiwin on the Calgary and Edmonton line. But the Canadian Pacific's first thought was to settle and develop the lands which were reasonably close to its main line, and, absorbed in this work, it gave little thought to the Northern Reserve during the nineties. Indeed, during much of the period the movement to the West was so small and the demand for land so slight as to leave even the main line belt and the Southern Reserve largely unsold. Under such conditions there was little incentive to make the outlays necessary for construction in the North, and, in the main, the lands were ultimately served by other lines of railway.

The establishment of these land reserves of millions of acres, far to the north and south of the main line of the railway, the logical result of the terms of the Syndicate Contract, which included the "fit for settlement" clause, combined with a flat grant of acreage, made the Canadian policy entirely unique. When the rush of settlers to the Canadian West began, bringing an unprecedented demand for land, the Government consistently encouraged the building of competitive trunk lines to the West, and, eventually, both the Canadian Northern and the Grank Trunk Pacific were built through the Northern Reserve. The Canadian Pacific Company was placed in the position, then, of having land not only far removed from its own lines, but actually tributary to rival railways. Railway competition was doubtless a desirable thing, but under such circumstances it did violence to the theory implicit in the system of railway land subsidies—that the railway company receiving the lands would promote settlement as a means of developing traffic for its lines. Every settler placed on the lands in the north meant business for the other companies, not for the Canadian Pacific. There was no reason, therefore, for any special effort to encourage immigration to that region, no urge to build up settlements which would benefit competitors. In fact, if there were an incentive in either direction, it was to delay the occupation of those lands until the cultivation and development of the government land in that area had brought about a sharp appreciation in the value of the railway sections. The zeal which the Company displayed in the work of settling the South was largely absent in the North, where ordinary business sense dictated a policy of waiting for the enjoyment of the unearned increment resulting from the labor and capital expended by others. The contrast between the low prices paid by the settler for land in the Canadian Pacific's forty-eight mile belt

and the high prices he was ultimately forced to pay for
that in the Northern Reserve is evidence that this waiting policy on the Company's part was, from the financial standpoint at least, entirely justified.

In the United States, where there was strict adherence to the principle that lands granted as subsidies
must be directly tributary to the railway, most efforts
towards holding the land for increased prices would
have resulted disastrously.   Here the generally accepted practice was for each railway to develop and
settle its own lands as rapidly as possible.   Even the
indemnity lands, located, as they were, not more than
fifty miles distant, could be included in such a scheme
of development.   The transcontinental companies,
building through unsettled country where traffic was
non-existent, were forced, in their own interest, to make
the rapid promotion of settlement one of their primary
duties.   They were likely to be mindful of the fact
that they were first of all transportation companies,
and only incidentally land companies, and that their
continued existence as transportation enterprises depended upon the increased traffic brought about
through the disposal of their lands to settlers.

The policy of granting Dominion lands without regard to distance from the railway was not confined
to the main line subsidy of the Canadian Pacific.   In
the late eighties, the Government, eager to expedite the
settlement of the West, offered additional grants to
the Company to encourage the construction of branch
lines in the South.   In 1889 provision was made for
a land subsidy in aid of the Souris Branch, which had
been located from a point on the main line near Bran-

don, in a southwesterly and westerly direction for about
185 miles.[34] At the rate of 6,400 acres per mile, the
construction of this road would entitle the Company to
about 1,200,000 acres.[35] Early in 1891, the president
of the Canadian Pacific expressed the willingness to
extend the Souris Branch to some lignite coal fields,
about sixty miles distant, in return for a grant of
6,400 acres per mile.[36] Since this extension would
place Winnipeg and the settled portions of Manitoba in
direct communication with a valuable supply of fuel,
and would provide railway facilities for an excellent
wheat producing region, the Government readily accepted the proposal.[37] An additional area of almost
400,000 acres was, therefore, added to the original
grant, making a total of more than a million and a half
acres to which the Canadian Pacific would acquire title
on account of the Souris Branch.[38] As in the main line
subsidy, the lands were to be "fairly fit for settlement." [39] The Company must pay $.10 per acre to
the Government to cover the cost of survey, and any
bona fide settler located on the lands was to have the
right to purchase from the Company as much as 320
acres at not more than $2.50 per acre.[40]

The insertion of the "fit for settlement" provision
in the grant precluded any possibility of finding in the
South the land with which to satisfy the subsidy, for,

[34] The history of this grant is to be found in *O. C.* No. 271, February 7, 1891.
[35] *Ibid.*
[36] *O. C.* No. 250, February 7, 1891.
[37] *Ibid.*
[38] *O. C.* No. 250, February 7, 1891.
[39] *Ibid.*
[40] *Ibid.*

as previously noted, there was not a sufficient amount
south of the main line to provide for the needs of the
main line grant.   Recourse must be had, therefore,
to the area in the North, to which the Company had
earlier relinquished its claims under the agreement of
1886.   Accordingly, it was arranged that the Company be given the odd-numbered sections in two strips
of twelve miles each on either side of the Battleford
Block, extending from Saskatoon, through Battleford,
and northwesterly to the 4th meridian.[41]   The area of
approximately 1,000,000 acres thus acquired would
be convenient for the Canadian Pacific to administer,
since the combined belts would extend twenty-four miles
on either side of this particular line of railway.[42]   To
satisfy the remainder of the grant for the Souris
Branch, there was reserved a triangular tract to the
southwest of the Battleford Block, an area of about
900,000 acres in odd numbered sections, from which it
was thought the necessary acreage could be obtained.[43]   In 1894, a further grant of 6,400 acres per
mile, authorized for the Pipestone extension of the
Souris Branch, again presented the problem of finding
increased acreage, and again resulted in an additional
reservation of land in the North.[44]   So, in return for
railway construction in southern Manitoba, the Canadian Pacific received lands in what later became
central Saskatchewan, an altogether significant com-

[41] *O. C.* No. 271, February 7, 1891.

[42] *Ibid.*

[43] *Ibid.*

[44] *O. C.* No. 253, February 10, 1899, gives the history of the grant
in aid of the Pipestone Extension.

mentary upon a very irrational feature of Dominion
land subsidy policy.

After the final reserve had been set aside for the
Canadian Pacific, a deficiency of some 3,000,000 acres
in the main line subsidy remained. Ultimate adjustment of the grant must depend upon agreement with
reference to a large area of land in the forty-eight mile
belt which was clearly not "fit for settlement." The
Company had not neglected opportunities for the development of the sub-humid portions of this belt.
Every acre of land which could be brought into the
"fairly fit for settlement" category meant an added
acre directly tributary to the railway. From Swift
Current west to the mountains the main line of the
Canadian Pacific traversed a region of deficient rainfall
—the home of the range cattle industry of Canada.
Here various experiments had been undertaken in the
hope that the country might be found suitable for grain
farming, and thus provide a greater volume of traffic
than that resulting from ranching operations. With a
view to determining the agricultural possibilities of the
section, the Company had established ten experimental
farms along the line west of Swift Current,[45] where all
sorts of field and vegetable crops had been planted.
Although the success of the experiments was strictly
limited by the climatic cycle, the farms were continued
for a number of years before they were abandoned in
the face of a capricious and fickle climate. Indeed,
so encouraging were the results first obtained that a
large German colony had been established at Dunmore
under the joint auspices of the Canadian Pacific and

45 *Manitoba Daily Free Press,* May 30, 1884.

the Dominion Government.[46]   But even the sturdy
German farmer had at last to admit defeat, and that
effort, too, came to naught.

Another very pretentious attempt at the development
of this semi-arid region was that of an English gentle-
man, Sir John Lister-Kaye.   It, likewise, failed, but as
an experiment in colonization de luxe it is most interesting.   In 1889 he presented to the Government a
petition setting forth his plan to settle seventy families
in each of twenty settlements along the main line of the
Canadian Pacific.[47]   He asked that he be allowed to
purchase at $1 per acre the quarter section contiguous
to the homestead of each settler, and that he be permitted to buy in connection with each colony 640 acres
in the center of the settlement, for the purpose of forming a community center.[48]   Each settler was to be
required to have 100 pounds clear, to which Sir John's
company would add, by way of a loan, $1,200, the
combined sums to be expended in the erection of a
"dwelling house, sheds for horses, cows, sheep and pigs;
and in the purchase of two mares, four cows, nine sheep,
four sows, share of digging a well, purchase of plows,
harrows, harness, seed-sower and seed.   From this fund
we also plough 20 acres, so that when the settler ar-
rives, as we intend him to do, June 1, 1890, he will find
his farm stocked and twenty acres in grain . . ." [49]
Thus would most of the difficulties of pioneering be removed!   The new arrival would find himself not only

[46] *Ibid.*
[47] The petition is with *O. C.* No. 208, May 27, 1889.
[48] *Ibid.*
[49] See the petition, *loc. cit.*

warmly housed, but spared the effort of turning the
first furrows in his new domain.

The expansive scheme of Sir John appealed to the
Canadian officials. The plan to settle 1,400 families
at different points in the Northwest Territories, combined with the prospective expenditure of $1,800,000
in the cause of colonizing the prairies, was too alluring
to be resisted, especially in a period when the movement
of people to the West had been all too slow. The plan
was given official sanction and operations on a large
scale were begun almost immediately.[50] The townships
for the experiment were to be selected, as far as possible, adjacent to the farms of the Canadian Agricultural Coal and Colonization Company, from Crane Lake
west to Langdon.[51]

Whether such an orderly and complete settlement of
a new country could have been carried out, even in
regions of consistent rainfall, is open to question. But
all the optimism of Sir John Lister-Kaye, the cooperation of the Government and the enthusiasm of the
early settlers were not enough to carry the project
through to success in a section of doubtful weather
conditions. The undertaking was a comparative failure and marked the end of large-scale attempts to
utilize the semi-arid region, in its natural state, for any
form of farming except stock raising.

Land which was suited only for live stock farming
could in no sense be regarded as "fairly fit for settle-

[50] *O. C.* No. 208, May 27, 1889.
[51] Ibid. This was another organization which had invested ex-
tensively in land at some nine or ten points along the C. P. R. main
line, in the dry belt.

ment," and unless some understanding could be arrived at between the Canadian Pacific and the Government with reference to the dry lands, it would be necessary to set aside still another reserve in the North, far removed from the main line. The only kind of agreement which would avail in this instance was one which would seek to adapt the policy of railway land subsidies to the conditions prevailing in that particular area. It was at this point that the Canadians developed a feature of their land grant policy which was vastly superior to the American policy, and which constitutes another important difference between the subsidy systems of the two countries.

Probably the greatest single weakness of the land grant policy in the United States was its inelasticity. Once the principle of the grant by alternate sections had been adopted, it had been impossible to depart from it, regardless of conditions. The alternate section idea had been established at the time when the energies of the country were engrossed in the settlement of the humid areas of the Mississippi Valley. There the alternate section was well conceived, and probably constituted the fairest method of dividing land between the railway and the Government. But, like the homestead unit of 160 acres, which was also the product of the fertile, well-watered regions of the West, the alternate section grant was totally unsuited to the semi-arid lands west of the 98th meridian. Some of the sub-humid country could have been reclaimed by irrigation, but no railway company could be expected to make the heavy expenditures for such a purpose unless the land was owned in solid blocks. On the other hand, most of the land in the area of deficient rainfall was valuable chiefly for grazing purposes. For efficient ranching operations, however, the 640 acre section was far too small a unit, and when rigorous adherence to the alternate section grant precluded the possibility of legal acquisition of large compact blocks within the limits of railway land grants, the cattleman was driven to the use of illegal means to achieve his objective. But the Congress which had waited forty-two years before attempting, in a feeble way, to adapt the homestead unit to the conditions of the Great Plains, was not disposed to bring the land subsidy policy into line with the needs and requirements of that region. In the face of such circumstances the Canadians were much more willing to experiment, and to adjust their policy to the special conditions prevailing in different areas. As will be explained later, the Dominion Government had in the decade of the eighties permitted deviation from the alternate section in the dry lands of southern Alberta.[52] Now, at the beginning of the next decade, it seemed that a similarly flexible policy with reference to the main line belt of the Canadian Pacific offered the best chance of effecting a final settlement of the Company's land subsidy.

Since such a large part of its land was located at a great distance from the railway, the Company was naturally desirous of locating within the forty-eight mile belt the largest possible portion of the balance due it. With this end in view, it was in the early nineties reexamining land which it had previously rejected as

[52] See pp. 90-92, *infra*. This was in connection with the subsidy to the Alberta Railway and Irrigation Company.

unfit for settlement.[53]   It was evident to the Government, however, that unless the alternate sections were abandoned, there was a great deal of the land which the Company would not accept.   In fact, the investigations of government agents confirmed the views of the railway officials as to the character of the land.   Early in 1894, the Deputy Minister of the Interior and the Superintendent of Mines jointly submitted to the Minister of the Interior a report in regard to the dry lands.   In this document they placed in writing the recommendations which they had made verbally "with regard to the relatively dry country along the line of the Canadian Pacific Railway which may be described generally as having its eastern boundary at Moosejaw and its western boundary at Crowfoot Creek, and within which during the past few years the rainfall has been insufficient to permit of the growth of cereal crops with reasonable certainty." [54]   Continuing, the report said:

There have been years within the experience of the Department when the rainfall was sufficient for this purpose, but such observations as we have been able to make during the years which have elapsed since the completion of the railway . . . would indicate that the recurrence of these dry periods is so frequent that while the country would in its natural state be well adapted for the grazing of cattle, the growing of cereal crops could only be rendered safe and sure by the application of an extensive and scientifically planned system of irrigation. The examination . . . of the physical conformation of the

[53] See letter of William Pearce, Superintendent of Mines, to John R. Hall, Secretary, Department of the Interior, December 1, 1893; File No. 211000-1.
[54] A. M. Burgess, Deputy Minister of the Interior, and William Pearce, Superintendent of Mines, to T. Mayne Daly, Minister of the Interior, January 29, 1894; File 211000-1.

country between Medicine Hat and the 5th Principal Meridian leads . . . to the conclusion that there are large areas in that region which could be satisfactorily and profitably irrigated by the waters of Bow River, and adopting the basis of calculation which experience in regard to irrigation would appear to justify, namely, that for every acre of irrigated land five acres of adjacent land would be rendered specially valuable for grazing and other purposes connected with the keeping and feeding of live stock, we have come to the conclusion that in round numbers about three million acres could thus be reclaimed from comparative aridity and rendered productive for all purposes of mixed farming, having special relation, however, to dairying and cattle raising.

The further observation was made that "in order to induce a Company organized on a thoroughly efficient financial and commercial basis to undertake the work of irrigating all or any of these tracts, it will be necessary that the sectional system of survey should be abandoned, that the road allowances provided for in the Dominion Lands Act should be closed up, that the area falling to the school endowment should be provided for in a solid block so situated as to derive reasonable advantage from the irrigation works, generally, and it would also be desirable that the Hudson's Bay Company should, if possible, be induced to . . . have their proportion of these tracts allotted to them on a similar basis. . . ." [55]

In other words, for the utilization of those lands irrigation was deemed necessary, and in order to induce a responsible company to undertake to make large expenditures for the purpose, the alternate section system of grants must yield to large, compact blocks. With

[55] Burgess and Pearce to Daly, January 29, 1894, *loc. cit.*

the opinion of the government agents, Sir William Van Horne, the President of the Canadian Pacific, fully concurred.[56]   He added, however, that the Company was not in a position to bind itself to undertake to bring the area under irrigation.[57]   All it could agree to do was to accept lands *en bloc* and take the chance that they might later be made available for settlement and cultivation by some scheme of irrigation.   Within limits, the Company was willing to take this chance. In fact, the Directors had passed a resolution authorizing Van Horne to accept lands in the district if conveyed in blocks. The President would look with favor upon an agreement binding the Company to accept a considerable quantity of land in large tracts, with the option of taking a larger amount within a stipulated time.   Such action he considered necessary, since the land would be worthless without water, and time would be required to determine the feasibility of irrigation.[58]

So satisfactory was the progress of the negotiations between the Government and the Company that in July, 1894, an Act of Parliament authorized the Governor in Council, with the consent of the Canadian Pacific Railway Company, to grant "so much of the subsidy lands of the said Company as remains ungranted, wholly or in part in tracts of such area as he deems expedient, and including sections bearing even, as well as those bearing uneven numbers, on that portion of the Main line of the said Company between

[56] W. C. Van Horne to T. Mayne Daly, Minister of the Interior, February 15, 1894; File No. 211000-1.
[57] *Ibid.*
[58] *Ibid.*

Medicine Hat on the East and Crowfoot Crossing on
the West, and within twenty-four miles on each side
of the said portion of the said Company's line of Railway.[59]   Sections reserved for the Hudson's Bay Company or for school purposes were not to be included
in the block, unless other public lands of equal extent
and value were provided elsewhere." [60]

It soon developed, however, that the terms of the
Act were not agreeable to the Canadian Pacific.   The
Company alleged that unknown to it the provision for
granting the lands *en bloc* had been made applicable
only to that portion of the line between Medicine Hat
and Crowfoot Crossing, and stated that after careful
investigation it had come to the conclusion that this
restricted area would not supply more than 1,000,000
acres of the deficiency in the main line grant, which
was in excess of 3,000,000 acres.[61]   Besides, it had
discovered that irrigation on a large scale would be
much less costly in proportion to results, and more
efficient, if carried out from the Bow River in the
neighborhood of Calgary than from any point within
the limits named in the Act of Parliament.[62]   When, a
few months later, the railway company formally with-
drew its proposition to accept lands in a block, its
action was based upon the belief that the powers given
to incorporated companies to take water from rivers in

[59] *Statutes of Canada,* 57-58 Victoria, Cap. 7, assented to July 23,
1894.
[60] *Ibid.*
[61] Charles Drinkwater, Secretary, C. P. R. Co., to T. Mayne Daly,
Minister of the Interior, November 26, 1894, Annex "B" to *O. C.* No.
3613, December 18, 1895.
[62] *Ibid.*

or near the territory in question, together with the authority assumed by the Government with respect to such waters, rendered it necessary that further details concerning the supply of water available for irrigation should be determined between the Government and the Company before entering into an agreement.[63]   The Company suggested, however, that there should be obtained an Act of Parliament giving the Government full power to deal with the problem, and expressed complete willingness to discuss the features and details of such an act.

Before an agreement had been reached, however, the Conservative Government was defeated in the election of 1896, and there followed several years of delay, during which no progress was made in the final adjustment of the Company's land subsidy.   The Canadian Pacific had been, of course, the creation of the Conservatives, and with the advent of the Liberals to power the close contact and understanding between Government and Company was largely destroyed.   During the early period of the Laurier Government the railway made few if any advances toward Ottawa, and certainly did not press for a settlement of the question of the land grant.   The Department of the Interior, engrossed in the formulation and execution of a vigorous policy for the promotion of settlement in the West, also gave scant attention to claims of the Company upon the Government.

The activity of the Government in advertising the attractions of the prairies to the farmer in the United

[63] Drinkwater to Daly, May 6, 1895, Annex "C" to *O. C.* No. 3613, December 18, 1895.

States, and the tide of immigration which began to pour into the Northwest at the beginning of the new century, made it the more important that the balance of the Company's lands should be located for them before it was too late. By 1901, informal negotiations had been resumed and two propositions had been made by the Government to the Company: one, that the railway should accept all lands within the forty-eight mile belt west of Medicine Hat, except Hudson's Bay lands; the other, that the area be extended considerably to the north and south.[64] In that same year the Company employed an expert irrigation engineer from the United States, who made extensive investigations into the problem of irrigating the district, and whose favorable report led to a continuation of the informal conferences. Early in 1903, the discussions entered upon their final stage, when the Company presented a very vigorous statement of its case. The Government, it was charged, had violated both the letter and the spirit of the Syndicate Contract by sponsoring a general policy of railway land subsidies which had made it possible for companies other than the Canadian Pacific to acquire much of the valuable land in the Northwest.[65] This policy had served greatly to restrict the area within which the Canadian Pacific might have made selections of land and needlessly complicated the problem of the ultimate adjustment of the subsidy. Reviewing the history of the land grant, the Company set forth in detail the

[64] Memorandum, William Pearce to R. E. Young, Department of the Interior, August 9, 1901; File 34187-14.

[65] Charles Drinkwater, Secretary, C. P. R. Co., to Clifford Sifton, Minister of the Interior, February 9, 1903; File 34187-14.

amount of land in the various reserves which came within the classification of "fairly fit for settlement."

	Acres
1. The Main Line Belt	5,255,870
2. The First Northern Reserve [66]	6,620,000
3. Southern Reserve [67]	2,244,130
4. The Lake Dauphin Lands [68]	400,000
5. The Second Northern Reserve [69]	386,000
Total	14,906,000

Deducting this figure from the 18,206,986 acres to which the subsidy had been reduced by the relinquishment of 1891, there was still due the Company an area of 3,300,986 acres. As yet no provision had been made for satisfying this balance. The lands in the forty-eight-mile belt west of Medicine Hat were worthless in their existing state. While it was conceded on every

[66] This was the area set aside by the Order in Council of October 24, 1882, and embraced the territory between the 52nd and 54th degrees of latitude and between the 110th and 116th degrees of longitude, from which, by the agreement of January 7, 1891, there was released the portion east of the 110th meridian, except for the Battleford Block.

[67] The area south of the main line belt, reserved by Orders in Council of November 3, 1882, and January 25, 1883. This was really in two parts. That reserved on November 3, 1882, was situated between the main line belt and the Manitoba South-Western Colonization Railway reserve, bounded on the east by the original western boundary of Manitoba, and on the west by the Coteau or Dirt Hills. The second part, reserved on January 25, 1883, was located between the main line belt on the north, the Red River on the east, the 49th parallel on the south and the original western boundary of Manitoba on the west.

[68] Reserved by Order in Council of February 18, 1895.

[69] Reserved by Order in Council of December 18, 1896, and situated between the 4th and 5th meridians (D. L. S.) and the 54th and 55th degrees of latitude. The region east and northeast of Edmonton.

hand that the irrigation of those lands would be of great benefit to both the Company and the country, it was estimated that it would cost about $3.50 per acre to bring them under water, which approximately equalled the average price received by the Company for its lands up to that time.[70] It could not think of accepting these lands, therefore, unless they were granted in a block. The odd and even-numbered sections between Medicine Hat and Calgary would amount to about 2,500,000 acres, which, if accepted, would still leave a balance of some 800,000 acres as yet unprovided for.[71]

The Company had observed that a considerable portion of the reserve set apart for the land grant to the Manitoba and North-Western Railway Company was no longer needed for that purpose, owing to failure to complete construction within the specified time. In this reserve there were some 1,200,000 acres in odd-numbered sections at the disposal of the Government, from which the Canadian Pacific would probably be able to select the remainder of its subsidy. Its proposal, therefore, was that it take the land between Medicine Hat and Calgary in a compact block and choose the balance from the Manitoba and North-Western reservation.[72] In submitting this proposition it recognized, of course, that should its scheme for irrigating the arid region prove a failure the lands would be virtually worthless.

Negotiations continued during the months which

[70] Drinkwater to Sifton, February 9, 1903; *loc. cit.*
[71] *Ibid.*
[72] *Ibid.*

followed, until by July 24, 1903, Clifford Sifton, Minister of the Interior, and Sir Thomas Shaughnessy, president of the Canadian Pacific, had agreed upon the essential features of a settlement.[73] The Company was to have practically all the land for which it had asked in connection with its irrigation project. It was to select in the First Northern Block any odd-numbered sections previously rejected but now considered "fairly fit for settlement"; and was to claim toward the satisfaction of the main line grant not more than 500,000 acres in the Manitoba and North-Western reserve. The Government would locate subsidy lands for the Saskatchewan and Western Railway, a small company previously acquired by the Canadian Pacific.[74]

Within a month the details had been worked out, and by an Order in Council of August 22, 1903, approval was given to the arrangement by which the main line subsidy, together with the subsidiary grants to the Saskatchewan and Western and to the Manitoba South-Western Colonization Railway, was finally closed out.[75] The Canadian Pacific agreed to increase to about 2,900,000 acres the compact area to be included in the irrigation project, and to accept in partial satisfaction of the bounty to the Manitoba South-Western a block of 100,000 acres of dry land in southern Alberta. To provide for the balance of the grant to this latter company, for the subsidy to the Saskatchewan

[73] Clifford Sifton to Mr. Turriff (Department of the Interior), July 24, 1903, File 34187-15.

[74] The grant amounted to only 98,880 acres.

[75] O. C. No. 1434, August 22, 1903. The grant to the Manitoba South-Western Colonization Railway had also been acquired and administered by the Canadian Pacific.

and Western, and for the residue of its main line grant, the Canadian Pacific might select not in excess of 642,000 acres in the reserve of the Manitoba and North-Western.[76] In this way there came into being the Irrigation Block of the Canadian Pacific in Alberta, where in the years after 1903 the Company undertook to develop perhaps the largest irrigation scheme in North America, as well as a program of assisted settlement and colonization far more extensive than anything which other land grant railway companies had attempted.

With the obligation of the Government to the Canadian Pacific discharged to the last acre, one phase of the Dominion subsidy policy was passed. The fundamental principles and practices which were developed in the handling of this grant for a large project became the generally accepted methods employed in the administration of subsidies for lesser undertakings. The features of the Canadian system which distinguished it from that of the United States were definitely established. The "fairly fit for settlement" clause had, in the main, been the force initiating these variations. The land reserves far removed from the main line of the railway, which resulted from the provision, were not easy to manage. The story of the subsidies to the smaller railways, which is the subject of the next chapter, will show the confusion and disorganization that often existed. In the United States, where the railway companies were forced to accept lands directly tributary to their own lines, regardless of quality, titles could be secured in a more systematic fashion. If the conse-

[76] *O. C.* No. 1434, August 22, 1903.

quences of Canadian departure from the American policy at this juncture seem not to have been too satisfactory, that was not true in other instances. The system in Canada was adapted and altered to fit particular situations in a way which was quite unheard of south of the border. When the need for irrigation demanded that the alternate section be abandoned in certain localities, the Canadians promptly abandoned it. By being willing to shape special points of a general scheme to specific needs, they avoided, to some extent at least, the difficulties which beset the Americans, who attempted to regulate the public domain from the Mississippi to the Pacific by the same iron-clad set of statutes.

CHAPTER III

The Extension of the Railway Land Subsidy Policy: the Grants to the Colonization Railway Companies

The land subsidy in aid of the Canadian Pacific, of course, in no way committed the Dominion Government to an extension of the policy of railway land grants. That railway was a national undertaking, whose very importance justified resort to extraordinary means to carry it through to a successful conclusion, and 25,000,000 acres of land was probably not an excessive price for Canada to pay for a transcontinental highway. Not only were there few who suspected that the land grant voted for one particular project would become the first step in the formulation of a general bounty system, but, doubtless, there were many who shared the point of view later set forth by the Canadian Pacific, that the encouragement of rival companies was not consonant with the spirit of the Syndicate Contract.

In the early eighties, however, the ambitions of aspiring capitalists, together with the local interest in railway building, brought forth a swarm of projected railway lines in the West. The Conservative Government, with a firm faith in the efficacy of the railway as an agency of colonization—a faith founded in part at least upon observation of the work of the land grant companies in the United States—gave generous aid, so that several of them were incorporated, received land grants and began railway construction.

The story of these colonization railways, as they were called, is all too often one of broken faith with the Government and of abuse of the land subsidy policy. Unlike the Canadian Pacific, which so faithfully complied with the terms of its agreement with the Government, these smaller companies, many times, merely wandered aimlessly out into the Prairie, arrived at no particular destination, and completed only a portion of their lines, but demanded the most considerate treatment at the hands of the Government. Determined to drive hard bargains with Ottawa, and frequently more interested in securing land than in operating railways, their every move was calculated to obtain the maximum amount of the best land, with a minimum expenditure of money and effort. The history of the subsidies to these companies, therefore, is replete with instances of non-fulfilment of contracts, with bitter controversy with the Government, and with prostitution for selfish purposes of what had once been a justifiable policy. The grant to the Canadian Pacific represented the subsidy idea at its best; those to the colonization railways illustrate the policy at its worst.

Particularly unfortunate was the application of the "fairly fit for settlement" clause to the subsidies of the colonization railways. While the inclusion of the provision in the Syndicate Contract could doubtless be defended on the ground of the great importance of the projected railway, no such argument could be advanced in support of the secondary railways. No other feature of the Dominion land bounty system is so difficult

to justify. Usually, the Acts of Parliament authorizing the subsidies were silent as to the character of the
land to be granted, but the companies, armed with the
Canadian Pacific precedent, presented their cases so
forcefully that the Orders in Council reserving the
lands stipulated that they should be "fit for settlement."
The clause was a prolific source of disagreement between Government and railways, and the disagreements
were the more prolonged because there was no satisfactory criterion of lands "fit for settlement" and no
tribunal to decide in cases of controversy. But if the
account of the subsidies to the smaller companies is
not a heartening one, it cannot, for that reason, be
omitted; for, taken collectively, the colonization railways constitute an important, if somewhat dubious,
chapter in the history of Dominion land subsidy policy.

The first gesture which the Government made in aid
of the colonization railways was not one of giving land,
but rather of selling it. The land regulations of 1879,
which had pledged 100,000,000 acres of the public
lands in aid of the Pacific railway, had divided the
land on either side of the railway to a width of 110
miles into five belts.[1] The even-numbered sections in
the various belts were to be available as homesteads and
preemptions, while the odd-numbered sections were to
be sold for the benefit of the railway, at a price ranging
from $1 to $6 per acre according to the distance from
the railway.[2] Shortly after the adoption of these regulations, the Manitoba and South-Western Colonization
Railway Company petitioned the Department of In-

[1] See pp. 15-17, *supra,* for a discussion of these regulations.
[2] *O. C.* No. 1422, October 9, 1879.

terior for aid either in land or money.[3]   This general
appeal for assistance was soon followed by the more
definite proposal that the Company be permitted to
buy government land; a first suggestion that it purchase 30,000 acres along their line of railway at $1
per acre being later displaced by a request that it
be allowed to buy from 2,500 to 3,000 acres of land
for each mile of railway constructed.[4]

The regulations of 1879, drafted as they were with
government construction of a Canadian Pacific railway in mind, clearly had no specific provision for the
sale of land to private companies engaged in lesser
undertakings.   But there seemed to be ample justification for an interpretation which would permit of the
sale of land to the Manitoba and South-Western Company and other small companies with similar aspira-
tions.   The Deputy Minister of the Interior, J. S.
Dennis, always a careful student of the land problem
in the West, had come to the conclusion that the sale
of land to companies of this type would be of mutual
advantage to the Government and the companies: to
the Government, because the construction of these lines
would open up to settlement the country at a distance
from the Canadian Pacific and thereby enhance the
value of the remaining government lands; to the companies, because of the fact that they could retail at a
profit the lands whose value had appreciated through

[3] See memo by T. G. Rothwell in regard to the land grant to the
Manitoba and South-Western Colonization Railway Company, December 17, 1883, File No. 21797-2.   In this memo the various applica-
tions of the Company for aid, beginning December 1, 1879, are traced.
[4] *Ibid.*

their own exertions.[5]   He recommended, therefore, that
the Manitoba and South-Western be permitted to purchase at $1 per acre 3,840 acres for every mile of rail-
way constructed, the land to be located within six miles
on either side of the line. The express provision was
made, however, that it could purchase in this manner no land in Belt A, the five-mile belt immediately
adjoining the Canadian Pacific. He further suggested that the Company be required to reimburse the
Government for the cost of survey and that the same
terms be extended to the Souris and Rocky Mountain
Railway and the Saskatchewan Valley Railway Company. Sir John A. Macdonald and Sir Charles Tupper, the Ministers of Railways and Canals, shared the
belief of Dennis, and in the summer of 1880 approval
of these proposals was given by Orders in Council
formally launching the Dominion Government upon
the course of selling land at $1 per acre to the so-called
colonization railways.[6]

But this new interpretation of Dominion policy in
regard to public lands was not allowed to stand without scrutiny and objection from the opposing political
faction. The proposed sale to the Manitoba and South-
Western was attacked in Parliament as in conflict with
the existing land regulations, and Sir John Macdonald, who had been in charge of the formulation of those
regulations, undertook to justify it. He pointed out
that land in Belt E, the farthest removed from the

[5] Memorandum by J. S. Dennis, Deputy Minister of the Interior,
to Sir John A. Macdonald, Minister of the Interior, June 23, 1880;
in Vol. 2, M. & S. W. Col. Ry. Co.; p. 774.

[6] See *Order in Council*, July 5, 1880, in Vol. 2, M. & S. W. Col.
Ry. Co., p. 773.

Canadian Pacific line, was in any event to be sold at
$1 per acre, so that the Manitoba South-Western "stood
in the same position as any private person choosing to
pay that price. This Company had no greater right
than any person in the world who chose to go and buy
in the odd-numbered sections, and it is of very great
importance to us that instead of individual speculators
going in, we should get a railway company to go there
and run a railway to these lands, thus increasing the
value of the lands in the even-numbered sections belonging to the government. Without a railway there
the land was to be sold at a dollar per acre, and it is
right that the government should give a preference to
this Company, which took a railway there, so that for
preemptions in the even-numbered sections the government would be able to get a higher price. It was an
incidental encouragement to this Company. . . . It
was not part of the proposal to make them a present of
the land, but we sell it to them at the same price as to
everybody else, as an encouragement to build the road.
. . . It is provided they should receive no land within
the Province of Manitoba, but they are to receive it
only in the district West of the Province." [7] By this
line of reasoning, the sale of land in Belt E to the
colonization railways, a procedure undoubtedly foreign
to the original intent of the regulations, was shown to
be not a violation of the existing land policy, but, on
the contrary, an integral part thereof.

The principle of selling lands to colonization roads
was accepted, but when the Government entered into
the contract with the Canadian Pacific Syndicate, by

[7] *Debates of the House of Commons,* 1880-81, p. 113.

the terms of which a forty-eight mile belt along the railway was created, drastic changes in these general land regulations became necessary. By Order in Council on May 20, 1881, new rules were issued, which divided the public lands for disposal in Manitoba and the Northwest Territories into two categories, those within the forty-eight-mile belt and those without.[8] This plan of division, after a trial of several months, was superseded by the more detailed plan of December 23, 1881,[9] which divided the surveyed lands of the Northwest into four classes. In Class A were the lands within twenty-four miles of the main line or any branch line of the Canadian Pacific.[10] Class B included lands within twelve miles on either side of any projected line of railway other than the Canadian Pacific. Lands south of the main line of the Canadian Pacific not included in Class A or B were placed in Class C, while Class D comprised all other lands. The even-numbered sections in all classes were to be held exclusively for homesteads and preemptions, with the exception of certain lands in Class D. The price of preemptions in the first three classes was fixed at $2.50 per acre, with those in Class D at $2 per acre.

A feature of special significance in the new regulations was that which provided that companies as well as individuals might, under certain designated conditions, enter into agreements with the Government for the purchase and colonization of portions of the public

[8] See *O. C.* No. 803, May 20, 1881, with accompanying memorandum by Sir John A. Macdonald, Minister of the Interior, dated May 18, 1881.

[9] *O. C.* No. 1710, December 23, 1881.

[10] *Ibid.*

domain. Lands granted for such purposes must be in Class D, and might be colonized under either of two plans. Under the first plan, the odd-numbered sections were to be sold at $2 per acre, with an added charge of $.05 per acre for survey charges, the entire amount payable one-fifth in cash and the balance in four equal instalments. The lands purchased were to be colonized within five years, the colonization to be accomplished by placing two settlers on homesteads on each even-numbered section within the area, each homesteader to have the right to purchase the preemption lot belonging to his homestead at $2 per acre. Should the settler on the homestead not elect to purchase the preemption, the colonization company might buy it at $2 per acre in cash. In return for having colonized the even-numbered sections in the block, the company was entitled to a rebate of one-half the original purchase money on the odd-numbered sections. This plan was in effect an inducement to private parties and companies to enlist their means and their energies in the cause of colonizing the West; as a consideration for settling the even-numbered sections, they were to be allowed to purchase the odd-numbered ones at a fifty per cent reduction. Under the second plan, both odd and even-numbered sections within a given tract in Class D could be purchased at $2 per acre in cash, plus $.05 per acre for the cost of the surveys. Within five years 128 settlers must be placed within each township, in return for which the company was to be allowed a rebate of one-half the purchase price.

Thus, these regulations of December, 1881, by making public lands available to companies organized purely for the purpose of colonization, created a new agency for the promotion of settlement in the West. The value of the colonization railway as such an agency had been generally conceded after the discussion in connection with the proposed sale of lands to the Manitoba and South-Western. In theory, at least, the spheres of the colonization company and the colonization railway were separate and distinct. While the regulations which planned for the colonization companies made no reference to the colonization railways, it is evident that any lands purchased by them would fall in Class B—lands within twelve miles on either side of any projected line of railway. The colonization companies, however, must take land at a distance from the railways, where, by virtue of the rebate allowed for fulfilment of settlement conditions, they could acquire land on the same terms as the railways, at $1 per acre. It is not without significance, though, that no conditions in regard to settlement were imposed upon the railway companies, probably because of the belief that need for traffic would supply sufficient incentive for them to encourage immigration into the Northwest.

Little use was made of the second plan of colonization as outlined in the regulations,[11] but great activity prevailed under the first plan. Numerous colonization companies were actually formed in accordance with this scheme, although popular fancy greatly exaggerated the number. Report had it that from 300 to 500 such companies had appeared, but the records show that less than 100 really existed.[12]   Sir John A. Mac-

11 *Debates of the House of Commons,* 1882, p. 810.
12 *Ibid.,* p. 809.

donald estimated in 1882 that the area of land to be acquired by the companies would not exceed 7,000,000 acres, and he reiterated his belief that by obtaining twenty or thirty colonization companies to settle and earn the land the Government was employing the most energetic mode of settling the country.[13]

The colonization companies quickly came under the fire of the Opposition in Parliament, and in Canada, as in the United States, charges of land monopoly and disregard of the rights of the actual settler were urged against them.[14] Replying to the criticisms of the Liberals, Sir John A. Macdonald asserted that in principle the plan for colonization companies constituted no new departure; that it was merely a continuation, in another form, of the policy which the Liberals had adopted in the seventies of encouraging parties to bring in immigration,[15] and that great care had been taken to prevent monopoly through the preservation of the homestead right of the settler. It was the hope of the Government that the colonization companies would "occupy the place for the present of the numerous railway companies in the United States, which have been proved there to be the best immigration agents—in fact, the only immigration agents in the United States." [16] Sir John was convinced of the necessity of having agencies interested in inducing and aiding settlement, and such agencies could not be expected to act from philan-

[13] *Ibid.,* p. 810.
[14] *Ibid.,* p. 803, for reply of Sir John A. Macdonald to this charge. See *ibid.,* p. 810, for question as to safeguarding rights of the homesteader.
[15] *Ibid.,* p. 803.
[16] *Ibid.*

thropic motives; they would interest themselves in land settlement only as business men, "just as the railways do, whose interest it is to get their lands sold and settled in order to obtain business for their lines." [17]

Events, however, were to prove that Sir John was over-sanguine in his expectations. Although concessions for colonization were granted to no less than twenty-six companies, for whom 2,842,742 acres of land were reserved for five years,[18] not one of the companies complied with the terms of the contract. Nine of them placed no settlers at all upon the land, while the others brought in a total of only 1,243 settlers. In the face of their failure an unusually generous Government granted them more than $320,000 as a compensation for expenses incurred in advertising, building saw-mills, and allowed the rebate on the purchase price of the land in spite of non-fulfilment of the settlement conditions. The companies acquired, therefore, a total of 1,421,371 acres at the price of $.85 per acre [19]—a sufficient reward for a doubtful service.

The reasons for the slight success of the colonization companies are not far to seek. In large part, these organizations were the product of the brief period of optimism, expansion and speculation in the West, which followed immediately upon the approval of the contract with the Canadian Pacific Syndicate in February, 1881. With Winnipeg in the midst of a real estate boom, with mushroom towns springing up on all

[17] *Ibid.*, p. 804.
[18] *Manitoba Free Press,* July 22, 1904, reviewing the history of the colonization companies.
[19] *Ibid.*

sides, and with visions of a headlong rush of settlers into the country, the wild lands of the West offered an irresistible attraction to investors organized as colonization companies. With the bursting of the bubble, however, there ensued a long period of disillusionment which blighted the fair prospects of the companies. It soon became evident that the Prairie must settle down for the long hard pull, and that the peopling of the Canadian West must await the passing of the choice lands in the United States.

While the colonization companies were proving comparative failures in the accomplishment of the objectives for which they were organized, there had been new developments in regard to the colonization railways. In fact, the more generous plans which had been adopted for these railways were used as an argument and a justification for the indulgent terms granted the colonization companies, notwithstanding their lack of success.[20]

The contract with the Canadian Pacific Syndicate had introduced the idea of free grants of land to corporations, and it was not surprising that as a result of this the colonization railway companies which had made prior agreements to purchase land [21] had become dissatisfied with their bargains. The people in the West joined the railway promoters in urging an extension of the subsidy principle to smaller companies. As the leading newspaper of the prairie expressed it: "Surely there is land and to spare in the Northwest, which cannot be put to a better purpose than the development

[20] *Debates of the House of Commons,* 1885, p. 92.
[21] See pp. 71-72, *supra.*

of the country. . . . Farming cannot profitably be carried on at any distance from a railway. In many of the prairie states of the American West the country is divided almost like a chess-board by railways; and farmers are seldom more than a few miles from a track. It would, of course, be unreasonable to expect as much for a new country like Manitoba; but there is no reason why we should be prevented from approximating it. . . ." [22]

The Government itself had implied a willingness to extend the privilege of free grants of land to the colonization railways, when in the spring of 1884 such a grant was made to the Winnipeg and Hudson's Bay Railway and Steamship Company.[23] In the face of the persistent popular agitation, an extension of similar subsidies to other companies was a comparatively simple accomplishment. In 1885, several of the colonization railway companies whose original agreements with the Government had provided for the purchase of land secured free title to approximately the same amount.[24] The subsidy principle by this procedure was made in effect retroactive, and there could be no further question as to the Government's interpretation of it.

In part, the popular enthusiasm for this general extension of the free grant to secondary railways was an expression of a growing lack of confidence in the colonization companies. Belief in the superior effectiveness of the colonization railway as an agent of

[22] *Manitoba Daily Free Press,* October 13, 1884.
[23] *Statutes of Canada,* 47 Victoria, Cap. 25, April 19, 1884.
[24] *Ibid.,* 48-49 Victoria, Cap. 60, July 20, 1885.

immigration and land settlement had grown steadily as
the consistent inability of the colonization companies
to produce any tangible results became increasingly
evident.   It was the colonization railway companies,
therefore, that ultimately came to be regarded as the
accredited agents for the development of regions not
reached by the Canadian Pacific, and as such the subsidies granted them and their final disposition are
significant.

Mention has already been made of the Manitoba and
South-Western Colonization Railway Company, which,
following incorporation by Act of Parliament in 1879,
had been authorized to build from Winnipeg in a southwesterly direction to a point near the western boundary
of the Province of Manitoba.[25]   By Order in Council
of July 5, 1880, the Company was permitted to purchase lands along its lines at $1 per acre and to the
extent of 3,840 acres per mile.[26]   Some months later
the Company asked for an increase of the acreage pur-
chasable, with the result that early in 1881 the amount
was fixed at 6,400 acres per mile, which thereafter
came to be the accepted area to which the colonization
railways were entitled.[27]   In 1884 Parliament gave the
Company power to lease its railway to the Canadian
Pacific Railway, thereby making it essentially a branch
line of the larger company.[28]   Later in the same year
W. C. Van Horne, of the Canadian Pacific, who was
also a director of the Manitoba South-Western Com-

25 *Ibid.,* 42 Victoria, Cap. 66, May 15, 1879.
26 See memo by T. G. Rothwell re Land Grant to M. & S. W. Col.
Ry. Co., File 21797-2.
27 *Ibid.*
28 *Statutes of Canada,* 47 Victoria, Cap. 73, April 19, 1884.

pany, advised the Department of the Interior that owing to the unfavorable impressions respecting the Northwest Territories and the prospects of the Canadian Pacific which had been created in England through statements circulated by a section of the Canadian press, the Manitoba and South-Western had been unable to raise the money with which to continue the construction of the line.[29] In view of the popular demand in the West for the building of feeders for the Canadian Pacific main line, the Minister of the Interior felt that the enterprise could not be permitted to go by default. He recommended, therefore, that, subject to the approval of Parliament, a free grant of 6,400 acres pere mile should be made to the Manitoba and South-Western for the whole distance between Winnipeg and Whitewater Lake, some 152 miles.[30] The necessary approval of Parliament was given, and the Government was confronted with the problem of finding and setting aside the land to which the Company would eventually be entitled.[31]

By 1891 the Company had constructed 212 miles of railway, which, at the rate of 6,400 acres per mile, entitled it to 1,356,800 acres.[32] Authority had originally been given, however, for a grant of only 960,000 acres, which had been earned by the construction of the first 150 miles of the line.[33] As the records of the Department of the Interior showed that the additional

[29] See facts stated in O. C. No. 1908, October 4, 1884.

[30] Ibid.

[31] Statutes of Canada, 48-49 Victoria, Cap. 60, July 20, 1885.

[32] O. C. No. 239, February 4, 1891. Ultimately a total of 1,396,800 acres was earned.

[33] This authority had been granted by Parliament in the Act 48-49 Victoria, Cap. 60, July 20, 1885, Statutes of Canada.

mileage had been built with the understanding that
the usual grant would obtain, and in view of the incal-
culable benefits which southern Manitoba had derived
from the construction of certain branches by the Company, the grant of 6,400 acres per mile was extended
to the entire line of the railway, making a total of
1,356,800 acres.[34]   The Company must pay the survey
fee of $.10 per acre, now a well established feature of
the land grant policy for the colonization railways.[35]

As in the case of the main line grant of the Canadian
Pacific, the task of locating and describing the lands
for the Manitoba and South-Western was rendered
more difficult by the inclusion in the Order in Council
providing for the grant, of a clause requiring that the
lands be "fairly fit for settlement." [36]   Prior to the
conversion of its option to purchase lands into a
free grant, a tract of land had been set apart, from
which the Manitoba and South-Western was to buy the
land at $1 per acre.   This area, known as the Inter-
national Boundary Reserve, stretched along the 49th
parallel between the road allowance separating Ranges
12 and 13 on the east and the Grand Coteau or Dirt
Hills on the west, and is not to be confused with the
reservation of similar name which had earlier been
established for the Canadian Pacific main line grant,
but which was situated farther to the east.[37]   When

[34] *O. C.* No. 239, February 4, 1891.

[35] *Ibid.*   The approval of Parliament was given by the Act 54-55
Victoria, Cap. 10, *Statutes of Canada.*

[36] *O. C.* No. 1908, October 4, 1884.

[37] See *O. C.* No. 239, February 4, 1891, which gives a resume of
the long history of the grant to the Manitoba and South-Western.
For the International Boundary Reserve of the Canadian Pacific, see
p. 38, *supra.*

the land subsidy to the Manitoba and South-Western was authorized, this reservation was continued as an area from which the subsidy lands were to be selected.[38]

The International Boundary Reserve, it was estimated, would provide in odd-numbered sections about 1,000,000 acres, leaving a very considerable residue to be found elsewhere. Since no lands were available in the vicinity of the line, it was necessary to locate them at a distance. As the Manitoba and South-Western had been leased by the Canadian Pacific, whose Land Commissioner would administer the grant, convenience and common sense seemed to require the reservation of lands which were contiguous to the main line belt of the Canadian Pacific. Accordingly, there was set apart a tract situated to the west of the 4th meridian and adjoining the forty-eight-mile belt on the south.[39] This block would yield about 465,000 acres in odd-numbered sections, which promised to satisfy the claims of the Manitoba and South-Western. Since this land was better suited to grazing than for ordinary agricultural purposes, the option of taking it in alternate townships instead of sections was given the Company.[40] Thus the railway received lands in what is now southern Alberta in partial satisfaction of a subsidy earned by virtue of construction in southern Manitoba. Obviously its line of railway was powerless to aid in the development of these lands.

Difficulty eventually developed, however, with ref-

[38] O. C. No. 1908, October 4, 1884.
[39] O. C. No. 261, February 5, 1891.
[40] Ibid.

erence to this tract of land. While the Canadian
Pacific had accepted prior to 1902, as "fairly fit for
settlement," about 1,000,000 acres from the International Boundary Reserve of the Manitoba and South-
Western, the Company had taken no steps to locate
the lands in the other tract. When the Department of
the Interior urged that the Company proceed with the
selection of the land in order that the grant might be
closed out as quickly as possible,[41] the Canadian Pacific, pressing for every advantage, chose adjoining
townships instead of alternate ones,[42] and ultimately
persuaded the Government to a reluctant agreement
to the procedure.[43] A new complication arose through
the discovery that prior to the reservation of this tract
for the Manitoba and South-Western in 1891, the
same area had been set apart for the land subsidy to
the Alberta Railway and Coal Company, and that
nearly three townships were included in the grant to
the latter company. The result was that when the
final adjustment of the Manitoba Company's subsidy
was made in 1903, at the time the main line grant of
the Canadian Pacific was closed out, only 100,000 acres
en bloc were taken in southern Alberta. To provide
for the balance, therefore, it was necessary to permit
the Canadian Pacific to select lands to the extent of
642,000 acres in the reserve of the Manitoba and

[41] Letters of James A. Smart, Deputy Minister of the Interior, to
Charles Drinkwater, April 9 and April 29, 1902, File 21797-4.

[42] P. G. Keyes, Secretary, Department of the Interior, to Charles
Drinkwater, October 14, 1903, File 21797-4.

[43] Drinkwater to Keyes, February 20, 1903, same file as above.
Drinkwater states he has taken the matter up directly with Minister
of the Interior, who approves of the adjacent townships.

North-Western Railway, in satisfaction of the Manitoba and South-Western subsidy, of the bounty to the Saskatchewan and Western, and of the main line grant to the Canadian Pacific.[44] Besides its dry lands in Alberta, then, the Manitoba and South-Western acquired an area far to the north of the Canadian Pacific main line. The American counterpart of this would have been a land grant in Colorado for construction in Missouri, or a subsidy in Arkansas for a railway in Iowa. It is not surprising, therefore, that Alberta has protested against the granting of her lands in aid of railways in Manitoba.

Of the various colonization railways probably none was of greater interest or importance than the Alberta Railway and Irrigation Company, which began as a coal-mining venture. At an early date coal had been found at the site of the present Lethbridge, Alberta, and while Sir Alexander T. Galt was Canadian High Commissioner in Great Britain he conceived the idea of mining the coal and transporting it by water to Medicine Hat, in what is now southeastern Alberta. With this in view, in 1882 the Northwest Coal and Navigation Company was chartered in England, with William Lethbridge as president and Elliott T. Galt as manager. It soon became apparent, however, that the idea of steamers pushing coal barges over the sandbars of the treacherous prairie rivers was most impractical, and that the streams which had been so well adapted to the bateau of the fur-trader were entirely unsuited to the more prosaic purposes of modern in-

[44] O.C. No. 1434, August 22, 1903. See p. 65, supra.

dustry. In 1883, therefore, Sir Alexander and his associates proposed that they build a railway from Lethbridge to Medicine Hat. Such a line, they alleged, was justified by the assured traffic in coal,[45] and by the prospect that the road would be the means of diverting to the Canadian Pacific the cattle and mining trade of Montana Territory in the United States.[46] By way of assistance in the execution of their plan, the promoters asked that they be permitted to purchase land at the usual rate of $1 per acre. Since the railway was to be a narrow gauge affair, provision was made for the sale to the Company of only 3,840 acres per mile, to be found in odd-numbered sections within a belt of six miles on each side of the line.[47] In 1885 the option to purchase the land at $1 an acre was transformed into a free grant of 3,800 acres per mile,[48] later increased to 3,840 acres.[49] An Act of Parliament in 1889 further increased the grant by 2,560 acres per mile for the 109½ miles between Dunmore and Lethbridge.[50] In the same year the group which was promoting this enterprise was incorporated as the Alberta Railway and Coal Company, authorized to construct a railway from a point near Lethbridge to the international boundary, and to acquire the North-

---

[45] O. C. No. 2147, October 19, 1883. In the memo of the Minister accompanying the Order in Council, the proposals of Sir Alexander Galt are set forth.

[46] Ibid.

[47] Ibid. The Company might also purchase 10,000 acres of coal lands, at the western terminus of the line, at $10 per acre.

[48] Statutes of Canada, 48-49 Victoria, Cap. 60 (1885).

[49] Ibid., 50-51 Victoria, Cap. 22 (1887).

[50] Ibid., 52 Victoria, Cap. 4 (1889).

west Coal and Navigation Company.[51]   A land grant not exceeding 6,400 acres per mile was authorized for this line to the boundary, a distance of 64.62 miles.[52]

The Alberta Railway and Coal Company absorbed the Northwest Coal and Navigation Company in 1891,[53] and with the growth of interest in irrigation in the southern Alberta country the sponsors of this company organized themselves, first as the Alberta Irrigation Company, and later as the Canadian North-West Irrigation Company. The corporate development of these various companies was completed in 1904, when the Alberta Railway and Coal Company, the Canadian North-West Irrigation Company and the St. Mary's River Railway Company were incorporated in a new organization known as the Alberta Railway and Irrigation Company.[54]

This Company earned a land subsidy of more than 1,000,000 acres by virtue of lines built by its predecessors, the precise figures being:

	Acres
North-West Coal and Navigation Company (First) Subsidy: Dunmore to Lethbridge, 109½ miles at 3,840 acres per mile....	420,480
(Second) Subsidy: Dunmore to Lethbridge, 109½ miles at 2,560 acres per mile	280,320
	700,800

51 *Ibid.,* 52 Victoria, Cap. 50 (1889).
52 *Ibid.,* 52 Victoria, Cap. 4 (1889), and 53 Victoria, Cap. 3 (1890).
53 See Preamble to 54-55 Victoria, Cap. 77 (1891).
54 *Ibid.,* 4 Edward VII, Cap. 43 (1904).

Alberta Railway and Coal Company
  (Third) Subsidy: Lethbridge to inter-
    national boundary, 64.62 miles at 6,400
    acres per mile 413,568
                                          ——————
        Total 1,114,368

The subsidy of the Company is of more than ordinary significance in relation to the Dominion policy of
railway land grants. Unlike the other bounties, that
of the Alberta Railway and Irrigation Company contained no stipulation that the lands must be "fairly
fit for settlement." Just why that clause should have
been omitted is not entirely clear. Perhaps it was because of the assumption that a company so peculiarly
identified with the semi-arid portions of the West must
necessarily accept lands not suited to ordinary types
of farming. Perhaps the interest of the Company in
coal-mining, grazing, and irrigation rendered attractive to it lands which did not fall in the category of
"fit for settlement." Of even greater interest is the
fact that it was in this subsidy that the Canadians first
departed from the alternate section method of allotting
railway lands, and began to adapt their policy to the
needs of particular areas—a departure which, as we
have seen, was carried far in the final arrangement with
reference to the main line grant to the Canadian
Pacific.

The Company soon discovered that, although the
land for six miles on each side of its line from Dunmore to Lethbridge was reserved for it, the odd-
numbered sections therein could not be obtained be-

cause they were included in the forty-eight-mile belt
of the Canadian Pacific—an interesting commentary
upon the confusion and lack of planning which so frequently attended Dominion land subsidy policies.[55] It
became necessary, therefore, to reserve lands farther
to the south and more remote from the railway. Moreover, for lands primarily suited to grazing, the alternate
section proved too small a unit to be disposed of ad-
vantageously. The Company asked, therefore, that
100,000 acres of the subsidy be conveyed to it in alternate townships rather than in sections, and that in the
case of townships fronting on rivers the latter should
be the boundaries of the grant.[56] The Hudson's Bay
Company was prepared to cooperate in such a consolidation by accepting its lands in that area in compact
blocks,[57] and of course the Government could take
similar steps with reference to school lands. As there
was then an active demand for land in large tracts for
grazing purposes, it seemed that the disposition of both
railway and government lands in the sub-humid region
would be facilitated by setting them apart by townships.[58] When the seal of government approval was
placed upon the plan, the first step was taken in the
conveying of subsidy lands *en bloc*.[59]

Meanwhile, the growth of irrigation in southern Alberta was preparing the way for further modification

[55] *O. C.* No. 1033, May 26, 1885.
[56] *O. C.* No. 1945, October 19, 1885. The Act 56 Victoria, Cap. 4,
gave the Governor in Council power to grant railway land subsidies
wholly or in part by townships.
[57] *O. C.* No. 1945, October 19, 1885.
[58] *Ibid.*
[59] *Ibid.*

of the original subsidy policy. Both the Government
and the Alberta Railway and Coal Company had become interested in the possibilities of irrigation from
the St. Mary's River, and in the summer of 1895 the
Department of the Interior had made extensive surveys with reference to a canal for that purpose.[60] It
was the consensus of opinion at that time, however, that
irrigation on a scale which would secure maximum
utilization of the water supply would have to be undertaken either directly by the Government or with
some form of governmental encouragement.[61] With
millions of acres available in the humid portions of the
West, it was unlikely that the Government would attempt such a work at that time. There was the danger,
however, that with delay, a number of small and waste-
ful irrigation projects might be constructed, thereby
consuming the water and leaving a large part of the
region incapable of irrigation. When, therefore, in
1895 the Alberta Railway and Coal Company made
known its desire to have a portion of its lands consoli-
dated into a block of some 500,000 acres, and expressed a willingness to proceed with the construction
of irrigation works, it seemed wise for the Government
to facilitate so far as possible such a plan.[62] With
this in view, an arrangement was effected whereby,
through an exchange of townships and parts of town-

[60] C. A. Magrath, Alberta Railway and Coal Co., to T. M. Daly,
Minister of the Interior, October 17, 1895, File No. 172441, in which
he refers to the surveys.

[61] Memo by T. Mayne Daly, Minister of the Interior, November
16, 1895, with *O. C.* No. 207, January 18, 1896.

[62] *Ibid.*

ships containing about 247,000 acres, a compact block of the desired size was obtained.[63]

In the face of the depressed conditions of the time the Company at first found it impossible to obtain the means necessary for reclaiming the arid lands. With the first improvement in the business situation, however, officials of the company went to Salt Lake City, where they entered into negotiations with the leaders of the Mormon Church.[64] The belief was that could arrangements be made with Mormon settlers for colonizing the lands, the means might then be found for financing an irrigation program. After numerous conferences a contract was made. The Mormons were to construct the canal system, payment for their labor to be half in cash and half in land at $3 per acre.[65] In consideration of the expense to be incurred in establishing the first settlers, the Company asked for a remission of the survey fee of $.10 per acre, a request which was readily granted by Ottawa, on the condition that within three years the Company should expend not less than $200,000 upon the work of reclamation.[66]

The project was pushed with vigor, and, as the canal system approached completion, the Company became desirous of effecting a further consolidation of the lands, with a view to bringing a larger portion of them within reach of the irrigation system. The Government

    [63] *Ibid.*
    [64] E. T. Galt to Clifford Sifton, December 15, 1897, File No. 172441-2.
    [65] *Ibid.* There is a copy of the contract attached to *O. C.* No. 3502, January 6, 1898.
    [66] *Ibid.*

looked with favor upon this proposal, too, and by further exchanges of townships the bulk of the lands of the Alberta Railway and Coal Company were made available *en bloc*.[67]

As the ambition of the Company grew, plans were evolved for the enlargement of the irrigation system. To this end the Government was asked to sell to the Company 500,000 acres of land at the price of $3 per acre, the figure named by the regulations for the disposal of lands for reclamation purposes.[68] The proposal was that the Company should be allowed a credit of $.60 per acre on account of previous expenditure for irrigation, and a credit of $1.40 an acre on account of the additional cost of extending the irrigation facilities, leaving a balance of $1 per acre—a total of $500,000—to be liquidated in ten equal annual instalments.[69] This plan, approved by the Government, enabled the Company to acquire control of the area commonly known as the 500,000 acre tract of the Alberta Railway and Irrigation Company.[70]

The agreement stipulated that the Company should not charge more than $5 per acre for this land and that any portion of the tract not sold within fifteen years should revert to the Crown.[71] This provision was evidently intended to prevent deliberate holding of the land with a view to appreciation in value, and it undoubtedly contemplated the sale of the land to actual settlers. Like so many government documents, how-

[67] *O. C.* No. 1995, August 17, 1900.
[68] *O. C.* No. 1858, December 12, 1902.
[69] *Ibid.*
[70] *Ibid.*
[71] *Ibid.*

ever, this one was not sufficiently precise and definite to preclude the possibility of conflicting interpretations.

Prior to the expiration of the fifteen-year period the Canadian Pacific acquired control of the Alberta Railway and Irrigation Company through the purchase of a majority of the shares of the capital stock. The two companies remained entirely distinct and separate, however, and in the early part of 1917 the unsold portion of the 500,000 acre tract was conveyed to the Canadian Pacific.[72] When the bona fides of this alleged sale, and its consonance with the spirit of the stipulation in the agreement of 1902, were challenged by the Department of the Interior, the Deputy Minister of Justice, while agreeing that the limitation upon the price of the land was designed to benefit the actual settler rather than the speculator, declared that it was impossible to impart to the clause a condition requiring that the land be sold within the limited period to actual settlers.[73] He was not prepared, therefore, to dispute the legality of the sale to the Canadian Pacific. History offers few better illustrations of clear conformity with the text of the law while doing violence to its spirit.

Few, if any, of the secondary railways showed more promise in the beginning than the Manitoba and North-Western, which began as a Manitoba corporation, under the name of the Westbourne and North-Western

[72] E. W. Beatty to E. L. Newcombe, Deputy Minister of Justice, July 13, 1917, File No. 3820437.

[73] E. L. Newcombe, Deputy Minister of Justice, to Controller, Land Patents Branch, Department of Interior, July 16 and November 27, 1917. File 3820437.

Railway.[74]   In 1882 the Dominion Parliament declared the projected railway a work of general advantage to Canada, endowed it with a Dominion charter,
and changed the name to the Portage, Westbourne, and
North-Western Railway Company.[75]   The following
year the road was acquired by men reported to possess
exceptional facilities for directing European immigration to the lands along the railway, and so successfully
was this fact exploited in the plea for governmental
bounty, that the Company was promptly permitted to
purchase 6,400 acres of land per mile for the entire
distance from Portage la Prairie to Prince Albert, the
price to be the usual one of $1 per acre.[76]   Shortly
afterwards the name was again changed—this time to
the Manitoba and North-Western Railway Company
of Canada.[77]

Construction of the first eighty miles of the line
proved costly, resulting in an expenditure of $1,-
600,000.   Difficulty was experienced in selling the
bonds of the railway, and although the Company was
certain that the enterprise would be a profitable one
ultimately, since the territory tributary to the line was
already well settled by people who had gone into the
territory in anticipation of the construction of the
Canadian Pacific by the northern route, it was faced
with the immediate need of raising funds.   Accordingly, it asked that the right to purchase land at $1
per acre be converted into a free grant.[78]   The request

[74] 43 Victoria (Man.), Cap. 41.
[75] *Statutes of Canada,* 45 Victoria, Cap. 80 (1882).
[76] *O. C.* No. 624, March 15, 1883.
[77] *Statutes of Canada,* 46 Victoria, Cap. 68 (1883).
[78] *O. C.* No. 1916, October 4, 1884.

was granted, and a subsidy of 6,400 acres per mile for a distance of 430 miles was provided.[79]

A tract of 3,368,960 acres was set apart and described as the area within which the Company might select the 2,750,000 acres to which this grant entitled it.[80] The reservation began on the west shore of Lake Manitoba, just north of the main line belt of the Canadian Pacific, and a short distance north of Gladstone. As it extended westward through Langenburg and Yorkton, the villages of Neepawa and Minnedosa were on the southern edge of the tract. Northwest of Yorkton, the belt widened out as far as Quill Lakes, only to contract again so that Humboldt was just south of the grant. Finally there was the broad area, north and south of Melfort, and stretching west until the western-most limit was almost coincident with a line south from Prince Albert. Within this last-named area was contained the Carrot River Valley, a region well known for its fertility. Taken as a whole, this reserve comprised a large area of the most attractive land in the West.

But even the land reserve was not enough to secure financial success. The Company was able to complete but 235 miles of the line, actually earning thereby only 1,501,376 acres of land.[81] The fiscal perplexities of the railway, in turn, brought no end of trouble for the Government. Early in its history the Company

---

[79] *Ibid.* The approval of Parliament was given in 48 Victoria, Cap. 60 (1885).

[80] See memo by A. M. Burgess, Deputy Minister of the Interior, to Clifford Sifton, February 27, 1897, File No. 377232. In this Burgess recounts the history of the land grant.

[81] *Ibid.*

adopted the policy of issuing land warrants good for 160 acres, to be applied on the land reserved for the railway. The Province of Manitoba, individuals, and corporations who gave financial assistance to the railway accepted these land warrants as security. In 1890, the Government of Manitoba, with a view to the more adequate protection of its investment in the railway, effected an agreement with the Dominion Government and with the Company, by which the Department of the Interior agreed to endorse these warrants as a means of affording more adequate security, and to patent to the Company or its assignees not more than 5,000 acres in any one month, without the consent of the Provincial Government.[82]   In accordance with the agreement, warrants for 1,452,320 acres were endorsed by the Department of the Interior and returned to the Company. When thus endorsed, the warrants could be located at the pleasure of the holders, with the result that there occurred inexcusable delay, which for years prevented the final adjustment of the land subsidy.

Equally serious was the question as to where the warrants were to be located. While the land reserved for the Company stretched away to the west and northwest for more than 400 miles, the railway was actually built for a distance of little more than 200 miles, and it seemed unlikely that the line would ever be finished.[83] Should the warrants be located in the area contiguous to the completed line of the railway, or within the whole area which had been reserved for the Company? This

[82] O. C. No. 787, March 31, 1890.
[83] Burgess to Sifton, February 27, 1897; loc. cit.

question was presented to the Department of the Interior in concrete form when the Manitoba and North-West Land Corporation, a company organized to exploit the land grant, forwarded warrants for more than 70,000 acres of which upwards of 50,000 acres were located in the Carrot River District,[84] far removed from the completed line of the railway. The Department refused to issue patents for the latter lands, and pointed out that there was plenty of land south of Township 30, Ranges 9, 10, and 11 west of the 2nd meridian. To this the Company replied that the Land Corporation had purchased warrants which stated that the holder could select 160 acres from the land grant reserved for the Manitoba and North-Western Railway Company, and that these warrants had been endorsed by the Dominion Government. In other words, the Company asserted the right to dispose of lands situated 200 miles to the west of its western terminus—lands which it had failed to earn by actual construction. Carried to its logical conclusion, the contention of the railway meant that from a tract of almost 3,500,000 acres it should be permitted, by shopping about from place to place, to select the 1,501,376 acres to which it was really entitled. To admit this right was to do gross violence to the theory upon which the policy of railway land subsidies rested.

This confusing state of affairs resulted from the fact that the Order in Council scheduling the Company's lands dealt with the entire subsidy and was passed upon the theory that within the time and on the conditions

[84] *Ibid.*

mentioned in the Order the railway would be built—a very unsafe assumption. Yet the Government was virtually powerless to correct the error. Much of the land had passed out of the hands of the Company and into the hands of private individuals and companies, who would have just grounds for complaint should Parliament do anything to derogate from the rights which they had innocently acquired. The offender was the railway company, not those who purchased the warrants. As a high-minded government official expressed it: "It does not seem to be quite right that this Company, a successful supplicant for merciful consideration at the hands of the government, should be permitted to pick and choose from land which was reserved as a subsidy for constructing a complete line of railway from Portage la Prairie to the Saskatchewan River." [85] This affair undoubtedly constitutes the most regrettable incident in the history of Canadian railway land subsidies, and the difficulties continued until 1903, when the grant to the Manitoba and North Western was sufficiently near final settlement to permit the use of portions of its reservation in partial satisfaction of subsidies to other companies, including the Canadian Pacific.[86]

Probably none of the railway land subsidies occasioned such bitter and prolonged controversy as that to the Qu'Appelle, Long Lake, and Saskatchewan Railroad and Steamboat Company. This company was incorporated in 1883, and arranged to purchase at $1 per acre 6,400 acres of land per mile for the twenty

[85] *Ibid.*
[86] See p. 65, *supra.*

miles of its line between Regina and the navigable waters of Long Lake.[87]   While a representative of the Company was in England in an effort to make the financial arrangements preliminary to the construction of the road, it came to his attention that other colonization railways had been granted land subject only to the payment of the survey fees.   He requested the same terms for his company, which were granted by Order in Council of December 30, 1884, the land to be "fairly fit for settlement." [88]   The following year Parliamentary approval was given to this grant,[89] and in 1887 a similar grant was authorized in aid of the extension of the railway to Prince Albert and Battleford.[90]

Between 1891 and 1902 four different tracts of land, aggregating approximately 4,500,000 acres, were reserved for the satisfaction of the subsidy of 1,625,344 acres actually earned by the Company.[91]   Of this amount 493,269 acres were retained by the Government for a period of years as security lands under an agreement entered into between the Company and the Government in 1890.[92]   On account of the chronically impecunious state of the railway in the early years, it became necessary for the Government to extend further assistance.   The latter covenanted to pay to the Company for twenty years the sum of $80,000 annually

[87] *Statutes of Canada,* 46 Victoria, Cap. 26 (1883).

[88] *O. C.* No. 2323, December 30, 1884.

[89] *Statutes of Canada,* 48-49 Victoria, Cap. 60 (1885).

[90] *Ibid.,* 50-51 Victoria, Cap. 23 (1887).

[91] For various reservations, see *O. C.* No. 234, February 4, 1891; *O. C.* No. 1635, June 10, 1892; and *O. C.* No. 1240, August 1, 1902.

[92] Such an agreement was authorized by the Act 52 Victoria, Cap. 5 (1889).   The agreement appears as schedule A of the Act 53 Victoria, Cap. 82 (1890).

for transportation of men, supplies, materials, and mails for the Government. As security, in the event the railway should fail to render that amount of service to the Dominion, the Government retained approximately 500,000 acres.

The history of the remaining portions of the subsidy is largely a story of disagreement. The men of the Qu'Appelle Company, more than those in other Companies, entertained an exalted conception of lands "fit for settlement," and to a greater degree, probably, than other companies, were determined to drive a hard bargain with the Government. In order to interest the banking house of Morton, Rose, and Company in the projected railway, the promoters, the well-known firm of Osler, Hammond, and Nanton, had assured the banking syndicate that the railway "would get a good selection of lands, and that the Government would treat the Company very liberally in this matter." [93] Indeed, according to the syndicate, they had been assured that they would be allowed "to select only such lands as we might consider favorable, both as regards quality and location." [94] Having made such glowing promises to their London correspondents, Osler, Hammond, and Nanton were firm to the point of insistence in pressing their claims in regard to the land grant.

By 1893 there had been reserved for the Company 2,743,591 acres, of which only 377,000 were acceptable to them.[95] Additional reservations were therefore

[93] E. B. Osler to Edgar Dewdney, Minister of the Interior, April 1, 1890. File 65383-3.

[94] John R. Hall, Secretary, Department of the Interior, to A. M. Nanton, April 21, 1893. File 65383-4.

[95] John R. Hall, Secretary, Department of the Interior, to A. M. Nanton, April 21, 1893. File 65383-4.

asked in the Swan River, Willow Branch, and Wood
Mountain districts.[96] The most the Government would
agree to at the time, however, was that, pending further consideration of the request for the lands in the
Swan River region, the Willow Branch and Wood
Mountain areas would not be granted to other companies.[97] This reference to the Swan River country
the Company chose to interpret as a promise that the
lands would be reserved for it, and threatened, in the
event of refusal by the Government, to send the reports
and correspondence to the London bankers.[98] Such a
procedure, the President intimated, would prejudice the
Canadian North-West in the eyes of the British, an
eventuality which the Government would want to avoid
at any cost.[99] A short time later this veiled threat was
made much more pointed, when another official of the
Company wrote to the Minister of the Interior that "if
this district in the Swan River Valley should be granted
to any other railway to the detriment of the Long
Lake, I feel sure that a blow would be given to Canadian credit in London that would be most serious.
The correspondence would be published in London, and
you can readily understand that in the present condition of financial affairs where almost all Houses are
smarting under various loses, the attack upon Canadian
credit and good faith would be most bitter. I should
be very sorry should such an event occur; but feel,
after carefully recalling all our interviews, and reading

[96] *Ibid.*
[97] *Ibid.*
[98] H. C. Hammond, President, Qu'Appelle, Long Lake, and Saskatchewan Co., to A. M. Burgess, May 3, 1894. File 65383-4.
[99] *Ibid.*

all the correspondence, that I have been perfectly justified in believing that it was the intention of the government to reserve the Swan Valley district for this Company, and I have submitted the correspondence to our legal advisers and they say that no other inference can be drawn from them." [100] A firm reply to this menacing letter drew another communication from the same official which can properly be described only by the word insolent.[101] The Minister of the Interior, in turn, unable to understand why the Swan River District was prized so much more highly than other portions of the West, chided the officials of the Company for coveting a region located at such a great distance from the railway.[102]

Examination by the government inspectors of the land already reserved showed that somewhat more than 1,300,000 acres were "fairly fit for settlement," as compared with 377,000 accepted by the Company's examiner.[103] According to William Pearce, a man renowned for his knowledge of land in the West, this Company's understanding of the words "fit for settlement" was far different from that of the Canadian Pacific and other companies receiving subsidies. Judged by the standards of the Long Lake Company, Pearce said, a large proportion of the cultivated lands of the Province of Ontario would be unacceptable.[104]

[100] E. B. Osler to T. M. Daly, Minister of the Interior, May 11, 1894. File 65383-4.

[101] Osler to John R. Hall, Secretary, Department of the Interior, May 21, 1894. *Ibid.*

[102] Hall to Osler, May 29, 1894. *Ibid.*

[103] A. M. Burgess, Deputy Minister of the Interior, to T. M. Daly, Minister of the Interior, June 11, 1894. *Ibid.*

[104] *Ibid.* Pearce was a veteran official of the Department of Interior.

The Minister of the Interior finally decided to stand by the report of the government examiners, even though the Company, in dissatisfaction, might litigate.[105]

Before legal proceedings had been inaugurated, however, the defeat of the Conservatives in the election of 1896 somewhat changed the situation. E. B. Osler, who had been the most persistent spokesman of the Company, was prominent in the Conservative Party, a fact which, no doubt, made it somewhat difficult for the railway to establish contact with the new Liberal Government. There ensued several years of inactivity, during which no progress was made in the settlement of the dispute. In 1900 Clifford Sifton, as Minister of the Interior, offered more favorable terms, which were rejected, and thereupon the litigation was actually inaugurated.[106] Before the legal issue had been decided, however, there appeared a group of American capitalists and speculators, organized as the Saskatchewan Valley Land Company, who were willing to purchase from the railway company the lands which the latter had rejected.[107] The manner in which this Company transformed 840,000 acres of land which had been condemned as worthless, and which were located in a region supposedly shunned by the settler, into a thriving and prosperous area will be related in another chapter (see pp. 124 ff.).

[105] *Ibid.* See marginal note of the Minister to that effect.

[106] For the important documents in this case, see Clifford Sifton to A. R. Creelman, January 25, 1900, File 65383-5. Petition of Right in Exchequer Court of Canada, January 31, 1900, *ibid.* Statement of Defence (in reply to Petition of Right) by E. L. Newcombe. *Ibid.*

[107] Memorandum by J. G. Turriff for Clifford Sifton, June 11, 1902. File 65383-6.

Among the last of the colonization railways to be projected was the Calgary and Edmonton, connecting the two most important points on the Prairie west of Winnipeg and opening up one of the choice portions of the western country. Prominent among the promoters of this enterprise were Edmund B. Osler and Herbert C. Hammond, who were also actively connected with the Qu'Appelle and Long Lake Company. By the charter, the Calgary and Edmonton Company was empowered to build a line between the two towns, with extensions to the Peace River on the north and to the International boundary on the south.[108] Provision in the charter for leasing or conveying the property to the Canadian Pacific suggests the possibility that from the beginning the Calgary and Edmonton had been intended as a branch line of the former company.

Shortly after the incorporation of the Company, the usual land grant of 6,400 acres per mile was authorized, the land to be located within a belt of twenty-two miles on each side of the line of railway.[109] While the Order in Council providing for the subsidy contained no "fit for settlement" clause, subsequent Orders scheduling the lands to the Company specified that they must be of such character. Although the creation of the twenty-two-mile belt along the railway line indicated an attempt to confine the land grant to the region tributary to the railway, as with virtually all the other subsidies, it soon became necessary to reserve other lands to supply the deficiency in the tract first set apart, a deficiency considerably increased by the fact that the

[108] *Statutes of Canada,* 53 Victoria, Cap. 84.
[109] *O. C.* No. 1655, June, 1890.

twenty-two-mile belt passed through the forty-eight-mile belt of the Canadian Pacific and through the block reserved for the latter company north of the 52nd parallel.[110]   For the most part, however, the additional areas were reasonably close to the railway line, in marked contrast with the remote reservations of other companies.[111]

As in the case of the Qu'Appelle, Long Lake, and Saskatchewan, the Government, in order to facilitate the Company in making necessary financial arrangements, agreed in 1890 to pay $80,000 annually to the railway for transport of mails, men, materials, and supplies; and by way of indemnity, should the services not amount to the sum paid, the Government retained 407,402 acres of the land grant—the lands thereafter being known as the Calgary and Edmonton security lands.[112]   When in 1903 the Canadian Pacific purchased control of the Calgary and Edmonton, the former became the successor to the interest of the latter company in the indemnity lands.[113]   This area was administered by the Land Department of the Canadian Pacific, while the balance of the 1,888,448 acres earned by the Company was conveyed to the Calgary and Edmonton Land Company.[114]

[110] *O. C.* No. 1979, July 8, 1893.

[111] *O. C.* No. 2787, Nov. 19, 1891, and O. C. No. 1979, July 8, 1893.

[112] *Statutes of Canada,* 53 Victoria, Cap. 5 (1890).   This agreement was to run for twenty years.

[113] H. C. Hammond, President, Calgary and Edmonton Ry. Company, to J. S. Turriff, Commissioner of Dominion Lands, November 6, 1903.   File 234347-7.

[114] Osler, Hammond and Nanton, Agents, Calgary & Edmonton Land Company, to Secretary, Department of the Interior, April 28, 1905.   File No. 234347-8.

Belonging to a somewhat different category are the land bounties in aid of several small companies which originally resembled the colonization railways, but which were ultimately lumped together as the Canadian Northern Railway Company. The subsidy of the latter company was really a compound of subsidies to three separate companies. One of these originated in 1883, when two companies previously organized were merged as the Winnipeg and Hudson Bay Railway and Steamship Company.[115] A year later a free grant of land was authorized for the Company,[116] whose name was changed in the next decade to the Winnipeg Great Northern Railway Company.[117] A second component part of the Canadian Northern grant was that to the Lake Manitoba Railway and Canal Company. This railway was first chartered in 1889 [118] and was voted a subsidy of 6,400 acres per mile the following year.[119] Incorporated anew in 1892,[120] the charter was acquired

---

[115] *Statutes of Canada,* 46 Victoria, Cap. 69 (1883). The original companies were the Nelson Valley Railway & Transportation Company, incorporated by the Act 43 Victoria, Cap. 57 (1880), and the Winnipeg and Hudson's Bay Railway and Steamship Company, incorporated by Act 43 Victoria, Cap. 59 (1880).

[116] *Statutes of Canada,* 47 Victoria, Cap. 25 (1884).

[117] *Ibid.,* 57-58 Victoria, Cap. 94 (1894).

[118] *Ibid.,* 52 Victoria, Cap. 57.

[119] *Ibid.,* 53 Victoria, Cap. 4.

[120] *Ibid.,* 55-56 Victoria, Cap. 41 (1892). The Company was authorized to build a line from a point in or near Portage la Prairie to deep water at the southern boundary of Lake Manitoba; also from some point on said line or from some point on the line of the Manitoba North-Western Railway, at or near Gladstone, northerly and northeasterly, and west of Lake Dauphin to a point on Lake Winnipegosis at or near Meadow Portage. In 1893 an Order in Council stipulated that the lands of the Company must be fairly fit for settlement. By the Act 60-61 Victoria, Cap. 49 (June 29, 1897), the Company was authorized to construct a line from Sifton Junction (then its terminus)

three years later by Mackenzie and Mann, who, in 1899, brought about the amalgamation of the Company with the Winnipeg Great Northern, under the name of the Canadian Northern Railway.[121] A third source of the Canadian Northern land grant was the subsidy to the Manitoba and South-Eastern Railway Company. Chartered in 1889, this Company was empowered to build from Winnipeg, in a southeasterly direction to the International Boundary,[122] and a year later was given the customary grant of 6,400 acres of land per mile.[123] By an agreement of April 28, 1900, confirmed by Act of Parliament the following year, the Company was merged with the Canadian Northern Railway, thereby completing the basis of the subsidy to the latter Company.[124]

The merging of these three small companies as the Canadian Northern Railway was merely the initial achievement in the careers of two of the most romantic figures in the annals of Canadian railroading. William Mackenzie and Donald Mann, both natives of Ontario, had advanced by way of the lumber camp to the dignity of railway contractors, in which rôle, working individually, they had engaged in construction work for the Canadian Pacific. Forming the partnership of Mackenzie and Mann in 1889, they had ob-

in a northerly direction to the south bank of the Saskatchewan. Also a branch from a point on the Company's main line near Dauphin, through Gilbert Plains, and thence to Shell River.

121 *Ibid.*, 62-63 Victoria, Cap. 57 (1899).

122 *Ibid.*, 52 Victoria, Cap. 60 (1899).

123 *Ibid.*, 53 Victoria, Cap. 4 (1890). By Order in Council of October 19, 1891, it was stipulated that the land should be fairly fit for settlement.

124 *Ibid.*, 1 Edward VII, Cap. 52 (1901).

tained contracts for the building of a number of railways on the Prairie and in other parts of the Dominion,
which absorbed their energies for several years. In
the course of this work they developed aptitudes which
were to fit them admirably for their subsequent careers
as railway promoters, aptitudes which so supplemented
each other as to make Mackenzie and Mann quite as
remarkable a combination as the "Big Four" of the
Central Pacific. Mackenzie became skilled as a finan-
cier, Mann as a manipulator of politicians.

Entering the game of railway promotion in 1895,
with the acquisition of the rights of the Lake Manitoba
Railway and Canal Company, which they soon con-
solidated with the Winnipeg Great Northern and the
Manitoba and South-Eastern, Mackenzie and Mann
had by 1900 laid the basis of an important railway
system on the prairies. Eventually they conceived the
idea of extending the Canadian Northern to the Pacific, and by means of money subsidies from the Government, by the sale of bonds guaranteed by the
Government, and by issuing to themselves virtually all
the common stock of the Company, they planned to
achieve, and did achieve, the impossible—the construction and control of "ten thousand miles of railway
without themselves investing a dollar." Such were the
men who now controlled the Canadian Northern, and
with whom the Government must deal in administering
the land subsidy which that railway had acquired from
the parent companies.

The policy of the Government in dealing with these
grants was attended by much of the confusion, as well
as a great deal of the leniency, which characterized land

subsidies generally. Probably no better example could be found of the insidious effects of the "fairly fit for settlement" idea than in connection with these bounties. The early Orders in Council in regard to the grants to the Winnipeg Great Northern and the Lake Manitoba Railway and Canal Company were silent as to the character of the lands to which the companies were entitled, but, in so far as the lands were to be situated within a stipulated distance from the railway, the presumption was that they need not be "fit for settlement." If, however, the officials of these companies were at first remiss on this point, they did not long continue so, and when the Lake Dauphin reserve for the Winnipeg Great Northern was created in 1895, the Order in Council contained the "fairly fit for settlement" clause.[125]   The following year a tract was reserved on similar conditions for the Lake Manitoba Railway and Canal Company.[126]   With the merging of the two companies as the Canadian Northern, and with the authorization in 1900 for Mackenzie and Mann to select land in the reserves of the parent companies,[127] those astute promoters seemed to be assured of lands of good quality.

As they were not the men to leave such matters to chance, they soon complained that the areas reserved would not provide sufficient land to satisfy the subsidies, and asked that they be permitted to select land in the reserves of other companies.[128]   In 1903, therefore,

[125] O. C. No. 464, March 5, 1895.
[126] O. C. No. 460, August 10, 1903, recounts the history of the grants.
[127] Ibid.
[128] Ibid. Reference is made to this request.

the privilege was granted to the Company of selecting 100,000 acres in the Manitoba and North-Western reservation, after which land might be claimed in the tracts set aside for the Qu'Appelle, Long Lake, and Saskatchewan up to December 31, 1905.[129]

Meanwhile, a controversy was developing between the Company and the Government as to whether the "fit for settlement" provision in the Order in Council of 1895, creating the Lake Dauphin Reserve for the Winnipeg Great Northern, applied to all lands to be earned by the Company, or merely to those acquired through construction south of the Saskatchewan River. Naturally, the railway chose the broad interpretation, and when the Department of Justice adopted the more restricted view,[130] the Canadian Northern, succeeding to the rights of the Winnipeg Great Northern, resorted to other and indirect means to obtain lands of high quality.

Although by 1907 the Company had selected 712,901 acres from the reserve of the Qu'Appelle, Long Lake, and Saskatchewan—an area greatly in excess of original expectations—it was determined to secure even further concessions from the Government. Through mistake, it was alleged, the Canadian Pacific had selected some of the land in the Lake Dauphin reserve, while the Government had dealt with the timber on a large portion of the reserve, either by permit or as berths, without regard to the rights of the Company.[131]

---

[129] *Ibid.*

[130] E. L. Newcombe, Deputy Minister of Justice, to Secretary, Department of the Interior, April 4, 1906.   File No. 505500-4.

[131] *O. C.* No. 1056, May 8, 1907.

Other portions were actually included in forest reserves or fell within the category of swamp lands and would be claimed as such by the Province of Manitoba. In view of these facts, therefore, the officials of the railway hoped for the continued indulgence of the Government. And the Laurier Government, which had staked so much on Mackenzie and Mann, could not well refuse. It was agreed, therefore, that the railway might continue to select lands in the reserve of the Qu'Appelle, Long Lake, and Saskatchewan, and in a block to the west thereof, contingent, however, upon the completion of the selection and the filing of the lists prior to August 1, 1907, when all unselected lands were to be released from reservation and thrown open to settlement.[132]

By 1907 the Canadian Northern had earned through construction under the stipulations of its different subsidies a total of 3,763,648 acres, while the completion of a projected extension of its lines would entitle it to an additional 238,080 acres, a total of 4,001,-728 acres.[133]   With settlement in the West proceeding

[132] *Ibid.*

[133] *Ibid.*   The amount earned under each subsidy was as follows:

Under the grant to the Winnipeg and Hudson's
Bay Railway and Steamship Company, later
the Winnipeg Great Northern—

	Miles	*Acres*
Beaver to Gladstone, and Sifton Junction to Provincial Boundary, all in Manitoba at 6,400 acres per mile................	171.70	1,098,880
Provincial boundary to Erwood in Saskatchewan, and from Erwood 70½ miles northerly at 12,800 acres per mile.....	92.66	1,186,048

For Lake Manitoba Ry. & Canal Company—

Gladstone to Winnipegosis	124.75	798,400

at a rapid rate, the Company was naturally desirous of effecting a final adjustment of its subsidy claims before the remaining lands were too much picked over. As yet virtually no progress had been made in locating the lands to which the Company was entitled through the construction of the Manitoba and South-Eastern line. The early Orders in Council with reference to this bounty had provided that the lands must be "fairly fit for settlement," but must be selected from lands east of the Red River.[134]   An Order in Council of July 31, 1897, however, had stipulated that if any of the lands reserved for the satisfaction of the Company's subsidy proved to be swamp lands to which the Province of Manitoba was entitled under the provisions of Section 1 of Chapter 50 of the Dominion Statutes of 1885, such lands should not be included within the grant reserved for the Company.[135]   Taking advantage of this provision, the Company had been able to find but 20,000 of the 680,320 acres it had earned, and it requested, therefore, that the Department of the Interior make arrangements for satisfying the claims of the Company.[136]   The Government agreed that in lieu of the

For the Manitoba and South-Eastern Railway,
St. Boniface, southeasterly to International
Boundary 106.30   680,320

                                              3,763,648

Completion of the line from the point 70½ miles north of Erwood to the Pas, a distance of 18.6 miles, would, at the rate of 12,800 acres per mile, entitle the Company to an additional 238,080 acres.

[134] O. C. No. 1060, May 8, 1907, which summarizes the earlier Orders in Council on the subject.
[135] Ibid.
[136] Ibid.

lands east of the Red River, the Company might select
land west of the 3rd meridian, on condition that it
should accept all the odd-numbered sections at the disposal of the Government in designated townships in
that region.[137]   Should additional lands be necessary,
the Canadian Northern could choose lands from the
reserve of the Winnipeg Great Northern, from that of
the Qu'Appelle, Long Lake, and Saskatchewan, or even
from a rectangular block situated to the west of the
latter reserve.[138]   Saskatchewan, therefore, was to re-
quite the claims of a railway line lying wholly within
the confines of Manitoba.   Here was revealed once again
the iniquitous workings of one of the most unfortunate
features of Dominion land subsidy policy—the granting of lands which bore no proper place relationship to
the railway which owned them.

The two smallest companies to receive subsidies were
the Great North-West Central and the Saskatchewan
and Western.   The former company was authorized
to construct a line of railway from a point on the Canadian Pacific main line, at or near Brandon, to the
Rocky Mountains, via Battleford, and was to receive
the usual land subsidy of 6,400 acres per mile of the
line between Brandon and Battleford.   Only fifty miles
of the railway were constructed, however, for which
the Company received a total of 320,000 acres.[139]   The
Saskatchewan and Western began as a Manitoba company, but in 1901 the Dominion Railway Act was

[137] *Ibid.*
[138] *Ibid.*
[139] *O. C.* No. 419, February 20, 1900.   This recites the entire history of the Company and its subsidy.

extended over it.[140]   For the construction of some fifteen miles of railway from Minnedosa to Rapid City, a subsidy of 98,880 acres was earned and subsequently taken over by the Canadian Pacific.   When in 1903 the final reservation of lands was made for the Canadian Pacific main line grant, provision was included for satisfying the Saskatchewan and Western bounty from the reserve of the Manitoba and North-Western.[141]

If the foregoing discussion has conveyed the idea that in the administration of railway land subsidies the interests of the railways frequently took precedence over those of the Government, that impression is likely to be strengthened by an examination of the policy with reference to mines and minerals.   Some of the land granted as subsidies to the railway companies was valuable for the mineral wealth it contained.   Particularly was this true of the grant to the Calgary and Edmonton Railway, which was rich in deposits of coal, oil, and natural gas.   While the rights of the Crown to lands abounding in gold and silver had been protected from the beginning, the policy with regard to those containing the baser metals had been less clear.   Finally, in 1889, regulations were issued by which the patents from the Crown for lands in Manitoba and the Northwest Territories reserved to the Crown all mines and minerals, with power to work them.

Since most of the subsidies ultimately earned had been authorized prior to the adoption of this rule, the reservation, of course, could not be wholly effective in respect to those grants.   The grant to the Calgary

140 *Statutes of Canada,* 1 Edward VII, Cap. 83 (1901).
141 *O. C.* No. 1434, August 22, 1903.

and Edmonton, however, was made subsequent to the ruling, and, when the Company claimed all mines and minerals, gold and silver excepted, the Government promptly pointed out that this was contrary to the regulations. There followed litigation, which the railway carried through the Supreme Court of Canada to the Judicial Committee of the Privy Council, where, on August 5, 1904, the decision of the Supreme Court was reversed.

In thus sustaining the contention of the railway, the Privy Council observed that "regulations relating to Crown lands reserved for sale or homesteads, have no application to the lands reserved for the totally different purpose . . . of subsidies for public works. . . . The lands in question are Dominion lands until parted with, but they cease to be so when granted to the Company; and none of the regulations relating to settlement, use and occupation of Dominion lands have any bearing on the present controversy. . . ." [142]

This decision enunciated a principle of far-reaching importance, of which other companies quickly took advantage. When later in the same year, therefore, the Canadian Pacific insisted upon the application of the principle to their Souris Branch, with the Pipestone Extension, the Department of Justice had no other alternative than to accede to the demand. [143]

As in the United States, so in Canada, railway land subsidies were at first hailed with delight, had their day, served their purpose, and ultimately called forth

[142] For all the documents in this case, see File No. 234347-8.

[143] E. L. Newcombe, Deputy Minister of Justice, to Secretary, Department of the Interior, November 16, 1904. File No. 775871.

a widespread popular disapproval. With millions of acres locked up in great reserves for the railways, and with settlement rapidly pouring into the West at the beginning of the new century, the opposition to land monopoly called a halt to further land grants, forced the cancellation of subsidies which had lapsed through non-construction of the railways, and brought about the era of aid to railways through governmental guarantees instead of land bounties. It happened that in Canada the rejection of the land grant policy synchronized with the advent of the Liberal Party to power in 1896.[144] As a result, there devolved upon them the task of closing out the subsidies which had been earned, and of forfeiting those unearned. In 1903 nearly 13,000,000 acres in lapsed grants were recovered by the Government,[145] while in 1907 the earned subsidies were finally located and the unused land in the railway reserves was opened to settlement. In the process of bringing to a close the land bounty period, ample opportunity was given to the Liberals to denounce the extravagance of the Conservatives and to pose as the friend of the poor homesteader who had suffered from the setting aside of millions of acres in reserves for the

[144] There is not wanting evidence to show that the Conservative Party was growing less indulgent in the matter before their retirement in 1896. A case in point is the firm attitude which the Department of the Interior took toward the unreasonable demands of the Qu'Appelle, Long Lake, and Saskatchewan Company. Even more significant is the abandonment of the "fairly fit for settlement" provision in 1894. In that year this clause was omitted in the subsidies authorized for the Wolseley and Fort Qu'Appelle Railway and for the Rocky Mountain Railway and Coal Company. For the documents in regard to this, see File No. 341086. Neither of these subsidies was earned.

[145] *Debates of the House of Commons*, 1903, p. 3798.

railways. In view of the demand for the development of the West by means of railways, however, it is difficult to see how any party in power in the eighties and early nineties could have resisted the land subsidy contagion; or how they could have stemmed the tide of disapproval of further grants which was running so strongly after 1896.

CHAPTER IV

Disposition of Lands by the Railways

No discussion of the railway land subsidy policy of the Dominion Government would be complete without some consideration of the methods by which the railway companies administered and disposed of their lands. With the example of the American railways in mind, Canadian opinion entertained high hopes as to the achievements of their own land grant railways in promoting settlement. In the final analysis, the vindication of the subsidy idea must depend largely upon the intelligence and sound sense of the railways in dealing with their lands.

Because the importance of Canadian Pacific land settlement policies requires a larger treatment which is to be accorded them elsewhere,[1] only brief mention is made of them here. The work of the other companies, however (which probably will not be made the subject of separate study), is discussed at greater length.

The Canadian Pacific, of course, was the first of the subsidized lines to formulate a plan for the sale and settlement of lands. The land regulations promulgated by the Company in 1881 were frankly an adaptation of those of the St. Paul, Minneapolis, and Manitoba Company, also controlled by the Canadian Pacific Syndicate. The essential feature of this plan was the

[1] The writer has in preparation a larger work dealing with the policies of the Canadian Pacific.

sale of land to actual settlers, with appropriate induce-
ments, in the form of a rebate upon the purchase price,
to those who would go into occupation of the land.   In
an effort to recruit settlers, a far-flung organization
was established in Great Britain, Continental Europe,
Canada, and, later, the United States.

While the Company sold much land in large tracts
to speculators, such as the sale of over 2,000,000 acres
to the Canada North-West Land Company in the early
eighties, and 1,000,000 acres to the North-West Colonization Company in 1902, together with smaller tracts
to other land companies, the fact remains, nevertheless,
that there was never a time when the officials of the
Company did not prefer to dispose of their land to the
bona fide settler.   And in most instances of conspicuous
departure from the principle of sale for actual settlement, peculiar circumstances or conditions played their
part; in the sale to the Canada North-West Land Company, it was financial necessity; in the case of the
North-West Colonization Company, it was the belief
that the enlistment of the aid of this important company, with large experience in land matters, would
facilitate the settlement of the lands tributary to the
railway.

If it was the well understood, though infrequently
expressed, policy of the Canadian Pacific to encourage
the occupation of the intervening government sections
in advance of the sale of its own, thereby securing a
higher price for its lands, the Company could always
point to the thousands of people carried into the Canadian Northwest, sometimes free of charge, sometimes
at nominal rates.   Tireless energy and an eagerness to

do everything possible to promote the growth and development of the country characterized this work.

In one respect, the work of the Canadian Pacific was unique among land grant railways in North America. Other companies sold land; the Canadian Pacific actually colonized it. In the 3,000,000 acre tract in Alberta it not only undertook to develop irrigation on a gigantic scale, but also attempted a most ambitious program of supervised and assisted land settlement. Starting in 1903 with the idea of encouraging the growth of a thickly settled area, based on irrigation and given over to stock raising and diversified farming, and finding its plans foiled by the ubiquitous speculator who refused to occupy the lands he had purchased from the railway, the Company gradually developed a scheme which included ready-made farms and loans to settlers, together with free instruction and training in the art of irrigation farming.

If the success of this venture was not all that the Company had hoped for, it was not due to any lack of effort, or to failure to appreciate the fact that the success of the railway as an agency of transportation was intimately bound up with a sound land policy. Beyond doubt, the fifty years of persistent work of the Canadian Pacific in settling the prairies justified the generous grant of land with which the Dominion Government had endowed the Company.

Of the colonization railway companies, the Alberta Railway and Irrigation Company probably more than any other pursued with reference to its lands a policy which fairly accorded with the theory that a railway receiving a land grant would be actively interested in the settlement and development of its lands. Given land much less attractive than that possessed by other railways, and which required irrigation to render it suitable for farming, this company was not only a pioneer in irrigation in the West, but also one of the successful agencies of land settlement. By the employment of American irrigation engineers, through contacts with the Mormon Church, and through the introduction of a considerable Mormon element into its territory, it exercised a far-reaching influence upon the whole course of development in southern Alberta. While the transfer of the unsold portion of the 500,000 acre tract to the Canadian Pacific in 1917 may, in a measure, have done violence to the spirit of the agreement with the Government, much of the harm was removed from the transaction by the fact that the Canadian Pacific had long since adopted the policy of selling lands only for actual settlement. Everything considered, the Alberta Railway and Irrigation Company did a valuable work.

Unfortunately, a less favorable view must be taken of the subsidies to the other railways. To administer a land grant wisely it was probably necessary that the railway be a legitimate common carrier; the carrying of goods and people must be its chief concern. Too often these small companies subordinated their function as railways to their landed interests, with the result that the lands were disposed of in the easiest way possible, and quite without regard to the manner in which the railway or the public would be affected.

An example of railway land policies at their worst is to be found in the disposition of the Calgary and

Edmonton land grant. Possessed of lands in one of the fairest portions of the West, this railway had an admirable opportunity to perform an effective work of land settlement. Yet, there is no evidence that the railway company did anything in the way of an active campaign to encourage the occupation of its lands. Instead, it transferred the land bounty, except for the so-called security lands, to the Calgary and Edmonton Land Company,[2] which appears to have been collusively organized, and then the firm of Osler, Hammond, and Nanton, who were identified with both the railway and the land company, acted as agents for the latter in disposing of its lands.

Many were the land companies organized with a view to the exploitation of railway lands. Generally speaking, they were of two sorts. The one type was largely inactive, spent little money, and carried on no campaign in behalf of increased settlement. Rather it preferred to profit from the work of other agencies. Over a period of years nothing would be heard from it. Then, when an active demand for land had been developed, the company would advertise through the press in an effort to attract the attention of the settler or investor who had been lured into the West through the efforts of others. It was to this category that the Calgary and Edmonton Land Company belonged.

The other type of land company acquiring railway lands was of an active and aggressive nature, possessed a highly-perfected organization, and waged its cam-

[2] Osler, Hammond and Nanton, Agents, Calgary and Edmonton Land Company, to Secretary, Department of the Interior, April 28, 1905. File 234347-8.

paign on a wide front, especially in the United States. Such companies undeniably played a prominent part in the rush of American settlers to the prairie provinces beginning in 1902. Conspicuous among the companies of this kind was the Saskatchewan Valley Land Company, which acquired the bulk of the land grant of the Qu'Appelle, Long Lake, and Saskatchewan Railway and Steamboat Company.

It will be recalled that a prolonged controversy had developed between the Government and this particular railway, the bone of contention being the quality of the land which had been reserved for the Company. Prior to 1902 no progress had been made in the settlement of the dispute, and litigation had actually been instituted by the railway when there appeared on the scene a group of American land speculators who were willing to purchase the land which the railway alleged was not "fairly fit for settlement."

The members of the Saskatchewan Valley Land Company, as these Americans styled themselves, were men of wealth and large experience in land and colonization affairs. A. D. Davidson, of Minnesota, president of the Company, and F. E. Kenaston, president of the Minneapolis Threshing Machine Company, had been interested in a company which had purchased 1,000,000 acres of land from the Northern Pacific.[3] Walter D. Douglas, of Cedar Rapids, Iowa, president of the Quaker Oats Company, and Robert Stewart, of Chicago, one of the largest stockholders of the latter organization, were also prominently connected with the

[3] See the proposal signed by these men, dated April 12, 1902. File 695671-1. Also *Manitoba Morning Free Press*, May 14, 1902.

Land Company, Douglas being vice-president. George F. Piper and E. C. Warner, of Minneapolis, together with G. C. Howe and A. D. McRae of Duluth were also among the important shareholders. A. J. Adamson of Rosthern and D. H. McDonald of Qu'Appelle were the resident Canadians interested in the project, but the other men named, Douglas and Piper excepted, were natives of Canada who had emigrated to the United States. The interest of those residing in the United States had been aroused through samples of grain forwarded by Adamson and McDonald, through information supplied by General Colonization Agent Speers, of the Dominion Government, and through the natural attraction which the splendid cereal crops of western Canada had for the Quaker Oats Company officials. With a capital of $3,500,000, the Saskatchewan Valley Land Company purchased 839,000 acres of the land grant of the Qu'Appelle and Long Lake Company at $1.53 per acre,[4] thereby giving evidence of its faith in a region whose reputation was so unsavory that it had been shunned and avoided by the settler. But it was not merely the railway lands which had been neglected; the intervening government sections were equally in disfavor, until finally the desolate aspect of the tract had become a matter of concern to Ottawa.

On April 10, 1902, J. Obed Smith, the Dominion Commissioner of Immigration in Winnipeg, wrote to Clifford Sifton, the Minister of the Interior, calling attention to the importance of the settlement of the area. Smith thought the land might be of interest to

---

[4] *Debates of the House of Commons,* 1904, p. 7056, statement by Clifford Sifton, Minister of the Interior.

Americans, and since colonization agents from the United States were seeking tracts of land on which to locate farmers, some special inducement might be offered them.[5] As he expressed it, ". . . the government would be justified in making almost any concession to colonization agents from the United States and elsewhere who would undertake to settle the free homestead lands within the said tract."

It seems likely that the Saskatchewan Valley Land Company had been in communication with Smith, and his letter to Sifton appears to have been designed to pave the way for the proposition of the Land Company. This latter proposal bears the date of April 12, 1902, and on the 25th of the same month C. W. Speers, the General Colonization Agent of the Government, submitted the Company's offer to the Department of the Interior.[6] He stated that this neglected area, stretching along the line of the Qu'Appelle, Long Lake, and Saskatchewan Railway for a distance of 115 miles, discredited the whole country. Speers reported that he had interested some American capitalists and manufacturers of linseed oil, experienced in colonization work, who believed they could grow flax to advantage on the land, and who, according to Speers, were prepared to bring from 800 to 1000 frugal German families into the district. But the Land Company desired to acquire a compact block of land, which was not possible through the mere purchase of the railway lands. It proposed, therefore, that it be allowed to purchase 250,000 acres of government land which would give it

5 File No. 695671-1.
6 *Ibid.*

a large area *en bloc*.   Following some counter proposals
by the Government, an agreement was arrived at on
April 30, 1902.

According to the contract entered into by the two
parties, the Government was to sell not more than
250,000 acres in even-numbered sections within the
limits of the railway land grant, the price to be $1 per
acre.[7]   A deposit of $50,000 in scrip was made by the
Company, to be applied on the last 50,000 acres earned
by the Company.   In return for the privilege of pur-
chasing this area of land at the stipulated price, the
Company must place twenty settlers on free homesteads in the even-numbered sections of each township,
and twelve settlers per township in the area purchased
from the Government.[8]   In other words, in each township twenty settlers must be located under the homestead law and twelve on sale land before the Company
could purchase the balance of the even-numbered sections.   As a guarantee against undue delay by the
Company, the terms of the contract were to be completed
within five years—two-fifths within two years and one-
fifth each year thereafter.   Thus, in its relations with
the Government, the Saskatchewan Valley Land Company was not unlike the colonization companies of the
early eighties.   By colonizing homestead lands for the
Government, the Company earned the right to purchase
the remaining government lands within the railway
subsidy limits.

7 *O. C.*, May 24, 1902.   File 695671-1.

8 The Order in Council authorizing the sale to the Company did
not take into account the fact that the Company could not sell these
twelve quarter sections because they had not earned them.   This was
discovered later.

The work of the Company was carried on with the greatest vigor. No time was lost in the creation of a vast organization, especially in the United States, and in the summer of 1904 it had 2,200 agencies scattered over ten different states.[9] It built two hotels within the colonization district, operated them without cost to the prospective settler, and supplied free livery service to enable people to inspect the land. During its first season the Company spent nearly $40,000 for advertising and conducted an excursion of some 200 representative men from the middle western states into western Canada.[10] At the Minnesota State Fair in September, 1902, agents of the Company distributed 30,000 copies of the *Minneapolis Journal,* containing a two-page account of the advantages and opportunities which the Northwest offered to American farmers. A similar work was performed at the state fairs in Michigan and Illinois. In February, 1903, advertisements of the Company were being carried in 24 newspapers in Iowa, 56 in North Dakota, 20 in South Dakota, 83 in Minnesota, 12 in Wisconsin, 15 in Nebraska, and 112 in Illinois. Many of these were full-page advertisements.[11]

In the face of this publicity the land which had previously been considered worthless, and on which there had been but one or two settlers, soon became highly desirable. Within a few months the Company had sold 100,000 acres of the railway land to a German

9 *Manitoba Free Press,* July 22, 1904.

10 A. D. Davidson, President, Saskatchewan Valley Land Company to James Smart, Department of the Interior, February 21, 1903. File No. 695671-1.

11 *Ibid.*

Catholic colony from Minnesota, and this same colony had taken up some 800 free homesteads beyond the limits of the tract covered by the agreement with the Government.[12] Before the expiration of the time specified in the contract, 1,682 settlers had been placed on the even-numbered sections, or 59 in excess of the number required by the Government.[13]

The Company sold at $8 to $12 retail the railway land for which it had paid $1.53 per acre, and the government land purchased at $1 per acre. At wholesale, in blocks of 10,000 acres, the land was priced at $5.50, subject to a discount of $2.50 an acre for cash. When sold on time, a down payment of $1.25 was required on the large blocks, while in the case of retail sales the Company received one-fifth in cash and the balance in five annual instalments at 6 per cent interest. In all cases the purchaser must pay a survey fee of $.10 per acre. Commissions were paid to agents at the rate of $1 per acre retail, and $.25 per acre wholesale.[14] The precise number of settlers brought to the lands, railway and government, it is probably impossible to determine. At the end of the first year's operations the president of the Company expressed the belief that 3,000 heads of families would be a conservative estimate of the work of his organization.[15]

Naturally, such a spectacular venture in land settlement was not unattended by complaint and criticism. One of the charges frequently brought against the

[12] *Ibid.*
[13] Statement by Auditor General, May 1, 1908. File No. 695671-5.
[14] File No. 695671-2.
[15] Davidson to Keyes, Secretary, Department of the Interior, September 2, 1903. File No. 695671-2.

Company was that its agents took unfair advantage of settlers by telling them that in order to secure free homesteads they must also buy land from the Company. The latter steadfastly denied the accusation, but admitted that real estate men engaged in retailing blocks of land purchased from the Company were guilty of such methods.[16]

The Conservative Opposition in the House of Commons found much to criticize in the agreement between the Government and the Saskatchewan Valley Land Company. Notwithstanding the fact that a Conservative government had authorized the land grants to the colonization railways, had sponsored the plan for the sale of land to colonization companies at $1 per acre in the eighties, and had accorded unusually favorable terms to those companies in the face of their failure, the Conservative leaders could find nothing to approve in the Saskatchewan Company. They charged not only that the Government was giving credit to the Company for those who had voluntarily settled in their territory, but also that a large portion of the entries reported by the Company were fictitious, and made by persons having no intention of occupying the land.[17]   The Government, so the Opposition alleged, had made a very bad bargain. It had sold at $1 per acre land which the Company was retailing at $5 to $10 per acre, and, what was far worse, had accepted payment largely in scrip instead of cash.[18]   Nor had it escaped the attention of the Conservatives that A. J. Adamson,

[16] Davidson to Keyes, Secretary, Department of the Interior, September 2, 1903.   File No. 695671-2.

[17] *Debates of the House of Commons,* 1904, p. 7036.

[18] *Ibid.,* pp. 7039-40.

prominently identified with the Land Company, was a Liberal candidate for the House of Commons. One Opposition member questioned the propriety of this candidacy, forgetting that E. B. Osler had been a Conservative member of Parliament when more than one company with which he was identified had received largess from a Conservative government, and that among the Osler companies thus aided was the very one from which the Saskatchewan Valley Land Company had purchased their railway lands.

Upon Clifford Sifton, the Minister of the Interior, largely fell the burden of repelling the Conservative attack. Replying to Opposition criticism of the low price paid for the land, he pointed out that the lands would have been homestead lands had they not been sold to the Land Company; that by virtue of their sale the Government was just $250,000 ahead; and that payment in scrip was of no consequence in view of the obligation of the Government ultimately to redeem the paper.[19] Continuing, Sifton contended that

As to the general features of the transaction, the operations of the Saskatchewan Valley Land Company, resulting from the acquisition of this tract of land, have been of immense benefit to the Northwest. If we had given the land to it for nothing, we would have received benefits ten times over in return. This Company has been exceedingly efficient as a colonizing agent. It has placed a lot of valuable settlers not only on this tract but on the remainder of its tracts. I can recall no feature of our colonization policy in the Northwest which has been attended with greater success than the efforts of this Company. Every one familiar with the district will bear me out in what I say, that on this land which was tenant-

19 *Ibid.*, p. 7041.

less for many years, we have a very large and thriving settlement which bids fair to grow not only in numbers, but in
wealth. . . ." [20]

While Liberal members of the House of Commons
were engaged in refuting the charges of their opponents,
the leading Liberal newspaper in the West could, with
pardonable pride, draw an invidious comparison between the pathetic failure of the colonization companies
twenty years before and the conspicuous success
achieved by the Saskatchewan Valley Land Company.[21]
It was at the time, and has continued to be, the boast
of the Land Company that it did more to advertise
western Canada than all other land companies combined
and that it was the most important influence in starting
the American invasion of the prairies.[22] While this
ex parte evidence must be accepted with very material
qualification, it seems certain that, after making all
proper allowances for abuses which were inevitably in-
volved in an undertaking of such magnitude, the Company was a most important means of focusing the
attention of the American farmer and investor on the
Canadian Northwest. Yet, the very success of the
Land Company is a condemnation of the Qu'Appelle
and Long Lake Railway, which, intent upon obtaining
an undue advantage, had steadfastly refused to accept
the land in that area. All that this group of speculators accomplished in the colonization of that region
could have been achieved by the railway, without taking

[20] *Ibid.*, pp. 7041-42.
[21] *Manitoba Free Press,* July 22, 1904.
[22] File No. 695671-1, Ref. 761660, A. D. Davidson to J. A. Smart,
February 21, 1903.

from the pocket of the farmer the profit which served to fill the purse of the middleman.

Of the remaining colonization railways, the Manitoba and North-Western promoters in their early years were fairly zealous in promoting the settlement in their territory, especially when the limited resources of the Company are considered. They were instrumental in settling several colonies on government land, and co-operated with the Canadian Pacific and representatives of the Dominion Government in endeavoring to start a movement from the United States to the West in the early nineties. In its colonizing, however, the Manitoba and North-Western made little effort to facilitate the occupation of its own lands. No definite land policy seems to have been formulated, with the result that the bulk of the subsidy passed into the hands of a limited number of persons or land companies. Thus in 1905 a total of 1,378,720 acres of the grant was in the hands of seven parties, including the Manitoba and North-Western Land Corporation, the Winnipeg Western Land Corporation and the Manitoba Government, who held 295,360 acres, 426,400 acres, and 542,560 acres respectively.[23]

The lands of the Manitoba and South-Western Colonization Railway were administered by the Canadian Pacific and under the same general policies as the lands of the latter company. The 98,880 acre grant earned by the Saskatchewan and Western was sold outright to the Saskatchewan Valley Land Company, while the 320,000 acre grant to the Great

[23] File 91,700-8. Memo by R. E. Young to Mr. Rothwell, Department of the Interior, March 16, 1905.

North-West Central was acquired by the Canadian Pacific and disposed of by that company.

The Canadian Northern land subsidy passed largely into the hands of large land companies who purchased for speculative purposes. In 1903 the group of men who controlled the Saskatchewan Valley Land Company announced that, under the name "Saskatchewan Valley and Manitoba Land Company," they had purchased the entire land grant of the Canadian Northern.[24] They offered for sale 2,000,000 acres of the "best wheat and flax lands in Western Canada" at from $5.25 to $7.25 per acre. William Mackenzie, president of the Canadian Northern, speaking of the transaction, however, said:

"It is not so much a sale as an arrangement to sell, to make sales. It is an aggressive system for colonization purposes. The idea is to place the land in the hands of actual settlers. The people mentioned in the dispatch handle land on a fixed basis but I suppose it would scarcely be considered a sale until sold. They had settled other tract and no doubt will be as successful with this. Heretofore we have sold the land ourselves to pioneers, but we have been building railroads and we believe the methods we are now introducing will have the best possible results." [25]

While the precise nature of the agreement is not apparent, there can be no doubt that the Land Company pushed the sale of the lands with all the energy which had characterized its handling of the lands of the Qu'Appelle and Long Lake Railway, and of the

24 *Manitoba Free Press,* June 8, 1903.
25 *Ibid.,* May 12, 1903, under Toronto date-line.

Government. By the spring of 1904 it had secured control of over two hundred townsites along the line of the Canadian Northern, involving an investment of $1,000,000.[26] In 1905 the Company was running land seekers' excursions regularly to the Carrot River and Big Quill Lake Plains, and was advertising free homesteads in those areas.[27] Along with its redoubled efforts in Canada went a corresponding increase in activity in the United States, Scotland, and England, where additional agencies were established.[28]

Although the home-seekers' excursions reveal a laudable interest of the Company in the "dirt farmer" upon whom the prosperity of the West must so largely depend, one should not infer that they were averse to selling to the smaller land companies. The lands were disposed of in large and small tracts, to the settler and to the speculator. Some of these speculative purchasers, in turn, conducted their land business on a large scale and took their toll from the bona fide settler. Thus the Canadian Northern Prairie Land Company, for example, was in 1906 selling at $9.50 per acre land which had once belonged to the Canadian Northern land grant.[29]

Colonization railways received about 12,000,000 acres of subsidy lands. In return for the land thus alienated by the Government, there were constructed in the Northwest about 1,700 miles of railway, much of it poorly built and equipped. While the grants which

26 *Ibid.*, April 23, 1903.
27 *Ibid.*, April 1, 1905-July 15, 1905.
28 *Ibid.*, April 23, 1904.
29 *Debates of the House of Commons*, 1906, p. 3109.

ultimately fell to the Canadian Northern contributed to the development of a main trunk line, the other lines were never of more than local importance. They were expected to justify themselves through their activity in promoting immigration and settlement. Yet, in most cases their financial affairs were from the beginning in such a precarious state as to leave them with no means with which to carry on active work of colonization. Instead of selling the land to the settler at a moderate price, therefore, they disposed of it in large tracts to the land companies, who exacted tribute from the farmer who ultimately acquired the land. A careful reading of the history of these railways forces one to the conclusion that the policy of the Government in subsidizing them was a mistake. A similar amount of land vested in one strong company would have supplied the railway competition which was so much desired, and would have enlisted in the cause of land settlement a strong and vigorous organization not unlike the Canadian Pacific.

APPENDIX

APPENDIX

A total of 56,087,072 acres of land were voted to railways, first and last.[1] Of this vast area the various railway companies earned the following amounts:

	No. of Acres
Canadian Pacific (main line)	25,000,000
Canadian Pacific (Souris Branch)	1,408,704
Canadian Pacific (Pipestone Extension, Souris Branch)	200,320
Alberta Railway and Coal Company	1,114,368
Calgary and Edmonton Railway Company	1,888,448
Canadian Northern (including grants to Winnipeg Great Northern, Lake Manitoba Railway and Canal Company, and Manitoba and South Eastern)	4,001,728
Great North-West Central	320,000
Manitoba and North-Western Railway Company	1,501,376
Manitoba and South-Western Colonization Railway Co.	1,396,800
Qu'Appelle, Long Lake, and Saskatchewan Railway and Steamboat Company	1,625,344
Saskatchewan and Western	98,880
Total	38,555,968

Of the 38,555,968 acres earned, however, only 31,762,954 acres were actually alienated by the Dominion Government, since the Canadian Pacific relinquished 6,793,014

---

[1] *Debates of the House of Commons,* 1903, p. 2102.

140   APPENDIX

acres of its main line subsidy to the Government in accordance with the agreement of 1886.

Up to June 1, 1903, there had been forfeited through non-construction 12,865,232 acres,[2] and subsequently an additional 4,665,872 reverted to the Government for the same reason, making a total of 17,531,104 acres unearned out of the 56,087,072 acres authorized as subsidy lands.

2 *Ibid.,* p. 3798.

BIBLIOGRAPHICAL NOTE

BIBLIOGRAPHICAL NOTE

ORIGINAL MATERIAL

THIS monograph is based largely on materials in the Dominion Lands Branch of the Department of the Interior, in Ottawa. The more important documents illustrative of the railway land subsidy policy of the Dominion Government have been copied and assembled in nineteen large volumes, and were consulted in that form by the writer. The manuscript materials in the collection consist largely of letters which passed between the Department of the Interior and the railway companies receiving land grants, while the printed materials comprise the Orders in Council, with accompanying Memoranda, passed with reference to the various subsidies. Although some of this material may also be found in *Sessional Papers,* the records in the Dominion Lands Branch constitute the only complete record of the land subsidy policy of the Federal Government.

Aside from this collection, the principal original materials of an official character used in the preparation of the study were the *Statutes of Canada, Sessional Papers, Debates of the House of Commons, Journals of the House of Commons,* and the *Debates and Proceedings of the Senate of Canada,* all of which yielded data supplementing the documents in the Department of the Interior.

While a study of governmental policy in regard to land subsidies must necessarily rest upon official papers, newspapers are not without value as barometers of public opinion with reference to activities of the Government. The *Manitoba Free Press* is especially rich in comment revealing the attitude of the West towards land subsidies.

On the political aspects of the problem there is material in the *Memoirs of the Right Honorable Sir John Macdonald,* 2 volumes, Ottawa, 1894; and the *Correspondence of Sir John Macdonald,* London and Toronto, 1921, both edited by Joseph Pope.

Secondary Material

On a theme which has not been made the subject of special study, secondary works must necessarily be limited. There are, however, several works which indirectly throw light upon land subsidy policy and its background. Conspicuous among these are:

Dafoe, John W., *Clifford Sifton in Relation to his Times*, Toronto, 1931. Contains some material on the closing out of the land subsidies.

Innis, H. A., *A History of the Canadian Pacific Railway*, London and Toronto, 1923. This is an excellent work; while not primarily concerned with land subsidy policy, the book contains a good deal of material on that subject.

MacBeth, R. G., *Sir Augustus Nanton; a biography*, Toronto, 1931. Throws some light on the subsidies to the Calgary and Edmonton and the Qu'Appelle, Long Lake, and Saskatchewan Companies, also on the Saskatchewan Valley Land Company.

Parkin, George A., *Sir John A. Macdonald*, Toronto, 1910. Has data on political background.

Pope, Joseph, *The Day of Sir John Macdonald*, Toronto, 1920. Gives a brief discussion of the political situation in the seventies and eighties.

Saunders, E. M. (Editor), *The Life and Letters of the Rt. Hon. Sir Charles Tupper*, New York, 1916. Contains a discussion of the debates on the Syndicate Contract.

Skelton, O. D., *The Railway Builders*, Toronto, 1920. An excellent brief discussion of railway development in Canada; contains very little on land grant policy.

————, *The Life and Times of Sir Alexander Tilloch Galt*, Toronto, 1920. A good discussion of the Galt interests in southern Alberta, including the Alberta Railway and Irrigation Company.

INDEX

INDEX

Act of 1872, the, 7-10

Adamson, A. J., and the Saskatchewan Valley Land Company, 125

Alberta Irrigation Company, origin of, 88

Alberta Railway and Coal Company, land grant of, 85, 88; incorporation of, 87 88; irrigation projects of, 91-94

Alberta Railway and Irrigation Company, beginnings of, 86-87; corporate history of, 88; land grant of, 89-93; purchased by Canadian Pacific, 99; disposition of land of, 121-122

Allan, Sir Hugh, early connection with Pacific railway plans, 9; as president of the first Canadian Pacific Company, 10-12; correspondence of, 12

Allan Steamship Line, mentioned, 9

Angus, R. B., and the St. Paul and Pacific, 17

Atchison, Topeka and Santa Fe Company, expenditure of, 26

Battleford Block, the, of the Canadian Pacific, location of, 46

Beatty, E. W., mentioned, 94n

Blake, Edward, and opposition to the Syndicate Contract, 19

British Columbia, enters Confederation, 6; government control of lands in, 32

Burgess, A. M., Deputy Minister of the Interior, mentioned, 57n, 96n

Calgary and Edmonton Company, organization of, 105; land grant of, 105-106; purchase of, by Canadian Pacific, 106; and mineral lands, 115-116; disposition of lands of, 123

Canada North-West Land Company, and the Canadian Pacific, 120

Canadian Agricultural Coal and Colonization Company, mentioned, 54

Canadian Northern Railway Company, organization of, 109; land grant of, 109-110; disposition of lands of, 134

Canadian North-West Irrigation Company, origin of, 88

Canadian Pacific Railway Company, development of, 17-28; land grant of, 29-67; disposition of lands of, 119-121

Carrot River Valley, fertility of, 44

Cartier, Sir George, opposition of, to Act of 1872, 9

Colonization Companies, 74-79

Colonization Railways, grants to, 68-74, 79-118

Cooke, Jay, and interest in Canadian railways, 9

147